GROLIER
SCIENCE INVESTIGATIONS

HUMAN BIOLOGY

Investigations

GROLIER
SCIENCE INVESTIGATIONS

HUMAN BIOLOGY

Investigations

W. Michael Margolin

Vol. 1

Grolier Educational Corporation

Produced in the United States of America by Alpha Publishing Company, Inc., 1910 Hidden Point Road, Annapolis, MD 21401

Printed in the United States of America

First Edition

SERIES ISBN: 0-7172-7169-2

Library Of Congress Catalog Card Number : 91-077656

This *Human Biology Investigations* curriculum was designed for students who are not academically oriented and probably will not continue their science educations. The objective of this course is to prepare these young-sters to function in the adult world as scientifically literate individuals who will be able to make informed decisions about their lives, their family members, and the environment. Their ability to make these kinds of decisions will require a knowledge of basic biology.

This Human Biology Investigations curriculum is closely tied to practical biological issues. It can be used in its entirety as a one-year course in biology, or individual units can be extracted and used to supplement a life science curriculum or a less specialized biology curriculum.

The activities, demonstrations, and teaching strategies are designed to offer the teacher opportunities to infuse process skills, basic skills, and critical thinking skills into the curriculum. An important goal of science teaching is the development of process skills in our students. As a result of science education, students should be able to make observations, record data, manipulate data, and draw inferences. The student activities pro-vide students with many opportunities to learn and to practice process skills, e. g. , observing, data collecting, measuring, graphing, etc.

Because many of the youngsters who are in a nonacademic course are deficient in reading, writing, and computational skills, the student activ-ities are designed to offer opportunities for students to practice these basic skills and for teachers to reinforce them.

An important function of science education is the development of people capable of independent thought, able to make valid choices and to cor-rectly judge the assertions of people and organizations. If we hope to produce a generation of youngsters capable of independent thought, we must develop critical thinking skills in our students. In the student activity sheets and demonstration sheets and in the teaching strategies are many opportunities to develop and foster critical thinking.

Research has pointed to the importance of hands-on activities in science classes. It is important that we, as science teachers, provide our students with opportunities to learn science by engaging in the activities of science. The student activities in this book provide hands-on activities in which students can manipulate equipment, record and interpret data, and draw inferences and conclusions.

DA

As science teachers, we have the advantage of being able to present exciting demonstrations that stimulate interest in what we are teaching and help students understand concepts. Demonstrations, however, should not be used only for their motivational effect but should be an integral part of the lesson. The teacher who shows an exciting demonstration that is "magical" but does not relate to the topic he is teaching is not using a demonstration correctly. The demonstrations suggested in this book are directly linked to the topics being taught. To be effective, demonstrations should be appropriate to the topic being taught, visible to all students, well prepared, and practiced in advance by the teacher. In addition to their motivational attributes, demonstrations provide the teacher with opportunities to further the students' understanding of concepts, develop students' reasoning skills, and provide opportunities to think scientifically. The student demonstration sheets will help you guide your students through these demonstrations so as to maximize learning.

SCIENCE INVESTIGATIONS

Science Investigations is a series of science activity books designed to address the significant changes and reforms in 5–9 science education and child learning theories.

These books are written with the aim of promoting science education in middle schools. The activities included in *Environmental Science, Human Biology, Life Science,* and *Physical Science,* are intended to nurture the skills of students in laboratory techniques and critical thinking. These activities also provide opportunities to master a body of knowledge in a variety of topics.

The safe, interesting, and exciting activities included in this series are intended to enhance the middle school students' interests and attitudes toward science and help them become scientists.

Science Investigations also serves as a unique resource series for middle school school teachers. These books lessen the difficult task of collecting and assimilating information on many science topics. The brief review of biology, chemistry and physics and environmental science concepts are intended to strengthen the basic scientific background of elementary teachers.

The wide variety of choices of activities in this series offer equal opportunities for the average as well as the most gifted and talented students. The selected experiments include both easy and challenging experiments.

The Teacher's Section for each student laboratory activity and teacher demonstrations offers considerable background information for the teacher in understanding concepts, collecting materials, and discussion both before and after the laboratory activity. Many of the activities can be assigned as collaborative assignments with parents at home. Most of the laboratory activities utilize common materials, chemicals and simple equipment.

Mr. Kutscher, author of *Environmental Science Investigations,* is Science Chairman and Coordinator of Science Research for the Roslyn Schools, Roslyn, New York. Their science department, nationally recognized for excellence, emphasizes scientific processes through an independent research program as well as in its classroom activities. The philosophy of educational excellence in science is an actuality at Roslyn, and the activities incorporated into this book reflect that standard. It is exciting, easy to comprehend, and yet lends itself to concept development rather than to rote learning. Mr. Kutscher holds a B.A. and M.A. in Physics from the City University of New York. He has spoken on the topic of "How To Start A Successful High School Science Research Program" at the New York State School Boards Association, the annual meeting of the Science Teachers Association of New York State, and under the sponsorship of the National Science Supervisors Association, at the annual conference of the National Science Teachers Association. Mr. Kutscher is Chairman of the National Science Supervisors Association Environmental Education Committee, and is on the NSSA Executive Committee. He is a representative at the Alliance for Environmental Education. In addition, he lectures on nuclear and alternative energies, is active in Science, Technology and Society groups, and is on the National Board of Directors of Zero Population Growth. This year, he again conducted a National Science Supervisor Association endorsed workshop on high school science research at both the National Science Teachers Association annual meeting and the meeting of The Science Teachers Association of New York State.. He has presided and spoken about population, energy and other science technology society issues at national and regional NSTA meetings, professional growth day workshops, on television's "Straight Talk" and at the Edison Electric Institute's meeting for utility educators. Mr. Kutscher has been a science educator for twentyfour years, teaching environmental science, physics, astronomy, biology, chemistry, earth science and mathematics in all grades from seven through college.

W. Michael Margolin, author of *Human Biology Investigations*, is a personnel assessment specialist for the New York City public schools. Prior to this he was an assistant examiner for the New York City Board of Examiners, where he prepared and administerd examinations for teachers of science. His particular area of expertise is the development of laboratory performance tests. He holds a B.S. degree from St. Lawrence University and an M.A. degree from New York University. The author has been involved in science education in New York City for 29 years. For 22 of those years, He was a classroom teacher at Newtown High School, where he taught all levels of biology and chemistry. He has been involved in the preparation of curriculum guides for general science and chemistry.

Barbara Newman, author of *Life Science Investigations*, holds a B.S. in biology from Hofstra University and an M.S. in Science Education From Queens College of the City University of New York. During her nineteen years at Roslyn she has taught biology, chemistry, earth science, biochemistry, marine biology and laboratory technology, as well as serving as an advisor for students conducting research. She has written curriculum guides for the laboratory technology, life science and self–paced biology courses. Ms. Newman has helped to develop experimental state syllabi, has written questions for the National Science Teachers Exam, and has presented workshops at the annual meeting of the Science Teachers Association of New York State. Her broad experience was the basis for her selection to teach in the Roslyn School–Within–A–School program, which she did for many years.

Salvator Levy, author of *Physical Science Investigations*, has taught science in New York City and Roslyn since 1974. He holds a B.S. in Electrical Engineering from N.Y.U. and an M.S. in Physics and Education from Long Island University.

At Roslyn for 15 years, Mr. Levy has taught all levels of chemistry and physics, as well as physical science, astronomy, and earth science. Mr. Levy has also written the curriculum and laboratory activities for the physics program at Roslyn.

USING THIS BOOK

UNIT THEME: In each unit, the unit theme will help you define your objectives before planning your lessons.

TOPICS: Each unit is divided into topics. For each topic you are provided with a suggested time frame and scope.

TEACHING STRATEGIES: The suggested teaching strategies will help you determine the scope and sequence of the subject and to plan your lessons. Performance objectives are stated for each topic.

THE TEACHER'S GUIDE TO DEMONSTRATIONS for each topic describes demonstrations you can use in teaching the particular topic.

THE STUDENT PAGE for each demonstration provides you with handouts that you can copy for your students. These will help guide them through the demonstration and steer their thinking in the right direction. Some of the demonstrations are appropriate to the same topics and are duplicative. To provide you with a choice of the demonstration best suited to your particular needs, I have included more than one demonstration for certain topics.

THE TEACHER'S GUIDE TO ACTIVITIES will help you plan, assemble, and present the student activities.

THE STUDENT ACTIVITIES provide hands-on activities for your students that are directly linked to the topic being taught. The student activity sheets may be copied to give your students instructions as well as data sheets and questions to guide them to a correct conclusion and to help them understand the meaning of the activity. These sheets offer many opportunities to develop basic skills, process skills and critical thinking skills in your students. These activities are indicated by the symbol ✍ in the table of contents.

Table of Contents

Unit 4: How Do Plants Affect Humans?

UNIT 6: WHY SHOULD YOU VISIT THE DOCTOR'S OFFICE?

UNIT 7: WHY DO YOU BEHAVE AS YOU DO?

UNIT 8: HOW DO DRUGS AFFECT US?

UNIT 9: HOW CAN WE PREVENT AND CONTROL DISEASE

UNIT 10: HOW DO HUMANS REPRODUCE?

UNIT 11: WHAT DETERMINES WHO WE ARE? (GENETICS)

UNIT 12: HOW HAVE LIVING THINGS CHANGED? (EVOLUTION)

UNIT 13: HOW DO WE INTERACT WITH OUR ENVIRONMENT?

Student Page –
Crystal Growth

Name _____

Date _____

DESCRIPTION: In your own words, describe the demonstration of crystal growth.

_____

_____

_____

_____

_____

_____

_____

_____

QUESTIONS:

1. Because the crystals grew, are these crystals alive? Explain your answer.

   _____

   _____

   _____

2. How does the growth of a crystal differ from the growth of a person?

   _____

   _____

   _____

3. If growth is not always a characteristic of living things, is it correct to consider growth a life function? Explain.

   _____

   _____

   _____

   _____

Student Page – Classification of Living and Nonliving Specimens

Name _____

Date _____

DESCRIPTION: Write the name of each of the specimens in the appropriate place in the table below. Next to the name of each specimen indicate whether you think it is living (**L**) or nonliving (**N**)

Explain your reason for making each choice.

SPECIMEN	L or N	EXPLANATION

QUESTIONS:

1. How did you decide which things were living and which were not?

    _____

    _____

    _____

    _____

2. What did the living things have in common?

    _____

    _____

    _____

    _____

3. Were all of the nonliving things the same? Explain your answer.

    _____

    _____

    _____

4. Did all of the living things need oxygen? Justify your answer.

    _____

    _____

    _____

5. Do all living things perform their life activities in the same way? Explain your answer.

    _____

    _____

    _____

    _____

    _____

**Student Page –
Observation of Seeds**

Name _____

Date _____

DESCRIPTION: In your own words describe the seed package and its contents.

_____

_____

_____

_____

_____

_____

_____

_____

QUESTIONS:

1. Would you classify these seeds as being alive? Explain your answer.

    _____

    _____

    _____

2. Did you base your answer to question 1 on your own observations or on information about seeds that you had learned earlier?

    _____

    _____

    _____

3. Describe an experiment you could perform to test your hypothesis about whether or not the seeds are alive.

    _____

    _____

    _____

Student Page – Comparison of   Name _____
a Burning Candle With Respiration   Date _____

DESCRIPTION: In the chart below list your observations of the burning candle and what occurs during respiration.

OBSERVATIONS	
BURNING CANDLE	**RESPIRATION**

QUESTIONS:

1. In what ways is the burning of a candle similar to respiration?

   _____

   _____

2. In what ways is the burning of a candle different from respiration?

   _____

   _____

3. On the basis of your observations, is a burning candle alive? Explain your answer.

   _____

   _____

4. Describe an experiment that would help you learn more about the processes of burning and respiration.

   _____

   _____

Observation of Living and Nonliving Things

Name _____

Date _____

INTRODUCTION: The word *biology* means the study of life. Being able to define life and to recognize when something is alive are important tasks for a biology student. Before you begin this activity, make sure you can define the terms *alive, dead,* and *inanimate.* Distinguishing between things that are alive, dead, or inanimate is not always easy. In this activity you will be asked to decide which of these three categories various specimens belong in and to explain your decision.

EQUIPMENT AND MATERIALS:

> Various specimens provided by your teacher
> Hand lens

PROCEDURE: Your teacher has provided you with a variety of specimens. You are to decide whether each specimen is alive, dead, or inanimate and justify your choice only on the basis of your observations. In the data table below, record the name of each specimen, the category you are placing it in — (A)live, (D)ead, or (I)nanimate — and your reasons.

SPECIMEN	(A) (D) (I)	REASON

QUESTIONS:

1. Which specimens did you consider alive?

    _____

    _____

2. Do you see any similarities among the specimens you decided were alive?

    _____

    _____

3. Which life functions did you observe?

    _____

    _____

4. Which life functions did you fail to observe?

    _____

    _____

5. Why couldn't you observe all of the life functions that living organisms perform?

    _____

    _____

6. On what basis did you distinguish between things that were dead and inanimate things?

    _____

    _____

7. Define biology.

    _____

    _____

SUGGESTIONS FOR FURTHER STUDY:

- Make a list of the life functions common to all of the specimens you decided are alive.

Student Page –
The Need for Measurement

Name _____

Date _____

DESCRIPTION:

1. Below are two lines, labeled A and B

   A   >————————————————<

   B   ←————————————————→

   1. Which line appears to be longer?

   2. Using a ruler, determine which line is longer.

   The longer line is labeled _____ .

2. Describe the demonstration in which two volunteers put their hands into one bucket of water and then another. Record the actual temperature of the water in the middle bucket.

   _____

   _____

   _____

3. Your teacher has shown you several containers of water.

   1. Which container seems to hold the most water? Which container seems to hold the least water?

   _____

   2. What is the actual measured volume of water in each container?

   _____

QUESTIONS:

1. On the basis this demonstration, how would you rate our ability to make observations?

   _____

2. Why are tools important to scientists?

   _____

3.   List some tools commonly used by scientists.

_____

4.   Why is it important to use a thermometer to take a person's temper-
     ature if you suspect that he has a fever?

_____

5.   When following a recipe, why should you use a measuring cup?

_____

_____

Student Page –
The Crest Commercial

Name _____

Date _____

When Crest toothpaste was first released on the market, the commercials used to sell it were descriptions of experiments, supposedly performed, to prove the effectiveness of fluorostan, the fluoride contained in the toothpaste. In one such commercial, a study was described as follows: Students at a boarding school were divided into two groups. Members of one group were given tubes of Crest toothpaste containing fluorostan. Members of the other group were given tubes of the identical toothpaste without fluorostan. Both groups were given the same kind of toothbrush and instructions about how to brush their teeth. Both groups were encouraged to brush their teeth at the same times and were supervised in the dormitories to see that they brushed their teeth. Because they were at the same school they used the same water and ate the same food.

QUESTIONS: On the basis of this description answer the following questions.

1. What was this purpose of this experiment?

    _____

2. How were the tubes of toothpaste given to the two groups alike, and how were they different?

    _____

3. Why were the two groups given these toothpastes instead of two different brands of toothpaste?

    _____

4. Why were the groups given the same kind of toothbrush?

    _____

5. What was the advantage of doing this experiment at a boarding school instead of a school where students went home each night?

    _____

6. In this experiment, which was the control group and which was the experimental group?

    _____

7. How could you define a controlled experiment?

    _____

Student Page –The Observation of Three Colored Threads

Name _____

Date _____

DESCRIPTION: In the space below draw and label a diagram of the slide you observed of three colored threads.

QUESTIONS:

1. Were you able to see all three threads focused at the same time?

   _____

2. Explain why all three threads are not seen at the same time.

   _____

   _____

3. How does the fine–adjustment knob help you to observe the three threads?

   _____

   _____

4. On the basis of your observations, which thread is on top and which is on the bottom?

   _____

   _____

Student Page –
<u>What Is in the Box?</u>

Name _____

Date _____

DESCRIPTION:

1. On the basis of your observations of the box, estimate how many objects are in the box and what you think is contained in your box.

    Number of items in the box = _____

    Estimate of items in the box:

    _____

    _____

    _____

    _____

2. Describe what you did to determine the number of items in the box and what you think they are.

    _____

    _____

    _____

3. After learning from your teacher what the contents of your box were, how correct did you find your estimate to be?

    _____

    _____

QUESTIONS:

1. Were the observations you made of the box direct or indirect observations?

    _____

2. When do we make indirect observations?

    _____

3. Can you give an example of a time you must make indirect observa-
    tions?

    _____

    _____

    _____

4. On what did you base your guess of what is in the box?

    _____

    _____

    _____

5. Would you consider your guess of what is in the box a wild guess?
    Explain your answer.

    _____

    _____

    _____

    _____

Observation of a Burning Candle

Name _____

Date _____

INTRODUCTION: The ability to make clear, accurate observations is an important skill that a scientist must learn. In this activity you will observe a burning candle and record as many observations of it as you can. You must come up with a minimum of 15 observations but may find as many as 50. It is helpful for you to group your observations into three categories: observations of the candle, observations of the wick, and observations of the flame. You must record only observations and not interpretations of what you observe or assumptions about your observations.

EQUIPMENT AND MATERIALS:

> Candle attached to a can top
> Match
> Ruler
> Thermometer

PROCEDURE: Light the candle. Record as many independent observations of the candle as you can. You may use the ruler and thermometer to help you make the observations. You will find it helpful to group your observations into three categories:

> Observations of the candle
>
> Observations of the wick
>
> Observations of the flame

You should record at least 20 separate observations.

DATA TABLES:

No.	OBSERVATIONS OF THE CANDLE
1	
2	
3	
4	
5	
6	
7	
8	
9	
10	

No.	OBSERVATIONS OF THE WICK
1	
2	
3	
4	
5	
6	
7	
8	
9	
10	

No.	OBSERVATIONS OF THE FLAME
1	
2	
3	
4	
5	
6	
7	
8	
9	
10	

CONCLUSIONS:

1. Did you use any tools to help you make your observations? Which ones?

   _____

2. How did the use of tools improve your observations?

   _____

3. On the basis of this experience, how would you rate your powers of observation?

   _____

4. Are observations limited only to things you can see?

   _____

5. Draw and label a diagram of the candle.

SUGGESTIONS FOR FURTHER STUDY:

- Think of an experiment you could perform to see if a flame casts a shadow.

Using the microscope

Name _____

Date _____

INTRODUCTION: The compound microscope is one of the most important tools of the biologist. In this activity you will learn the proper use of the compound microscope.

EQUIPMENT AND MATERIALS:

> Compound microscope
> Light source
> Prepared slide of the letter *e*
> Lens paper

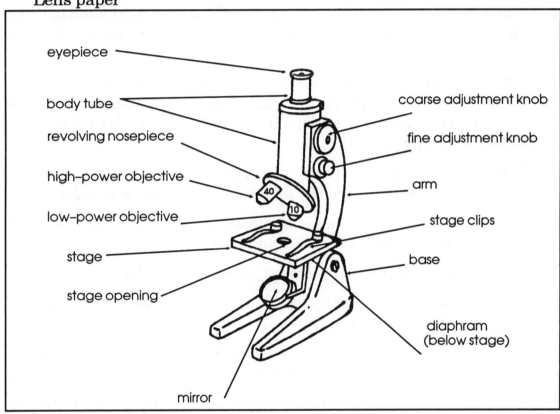

eyepiece

body tube

revolving nosepiece

high–power objective

low–power objective

stage

stage opening

coarse adjustment knob

fine adjustment knob

arm

stage clips

base

diaphram
(below stage)

mirror

Diagram 1-1 *Compound microscope*

PROCEDURE:

1. When instructed by your teacher to pick up your microscope, carry it with both hands, one holding the arm and one holding it under the base.

2. Place the microscope at your workstation so that the arm faces you.

3. Using lens paper, clean the eyepiece and objectives as well as the slide.

4. Turn the nosepiece so that the low–power objective slips into place (the low power objective is smaller and says 10x).

5. If your microscope comes with a substage lamp, turn it on. If your microscope uses a mirror to direct light into it, do the following: (a) If you have an external light, adjust it so that it directs light toward the mirror and use the flat mirror surface. (b) If you don't have an external light, use the curved side of the mirror to direct the light into the microscope. (DON'T use direct sunlight.) When you look into the eye–piece you should see a clear, bluish circle of light.

6. Place the slide on the stage so that the letter *e* reads right side up. Center the letter *e* over the opening in the stage. Hold the slide in place with the clips.

7. While looking at the stage, turn the coarse–adjustment knob to lower the objective as close to the slide as possible. Don't let it touch the slide.

8. While looking through the eyepiece, slowly turn the coarse–adjustment knob to bring the specimen into focus. If you turn the knob too quickly, you will miss the focus. If you do this, go back to step 7 and focus the specimen again.

9. Turn the fine–adjustment knob very slowly to bring the specimen into sharper focus. Do not turn the fine–adjustment knob very far.

10. Draw and label the letter *e* as it appears under the microscope. Don't draw it the way you think it should look.

11. Move the slide to the left. What happens to the letter *e*?

12. Move the slid up. What happens to the letter *e*? Before proceeding, make sure the letter *e* is in the center of the field.

13. While watching the stage, to make sure the objective does not touch the slide, turn the nosepiece so that the high–power lens is in place.

14. If you don't see anything under high power, switch back to low power, and make sure the letter *e* is directly in the center of the slide and in focus. Now turn back to high power according to the directions in Step 13.

15. Draw what you see under high power. Be sure to label your drawing — including the magnification.

16. When you have completed the exercise, remove the slide, turn the nosepiece so that neither objective is in place, and lower the barrel to the lowest position. Remember how to carry the microscope when you return it.

OBSERVATIONS:

Draw the letter *e* under low power.

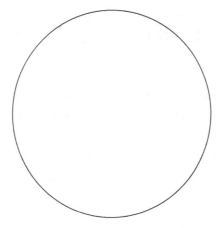

Draw the letter *e* under high power.

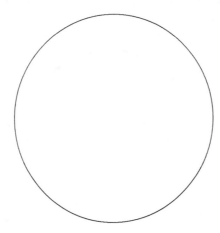

1.   When you moved the slide to the left, how did the letter *e* move?

   _____

   _____

2.   When you moved the slide away from you, how did the letter *e* move?

   _____

   _____

QUESTIONS:

1. Why must you watch the stage when lowering the low–power objective?

_____

2. Why is it so important to properly adjust the light before you begin.

_____

3. If the magnification of the eyepiece is 10x and the magnification of the high–power objective is 44x, what is the total magnification?

_____

4. Why is it important to label your diagrams?

_____

5. Why should you include the magnification when you label your diagrams?

_____

6. A student was looking at a specimen under low power as shown in the diagram below.

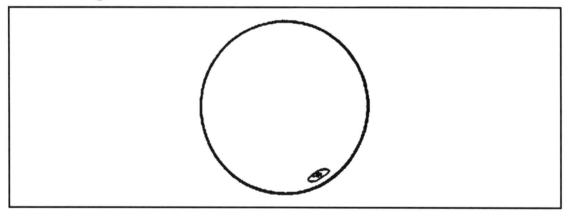

Diagram 1-2 _Specimen under low power_

What would the student see if he switched to high power? What could he do to correct this?

SUGGESTIONS FOR FURTHER STUDY:

- Get a slide of three crossed threads from your teacher. Look at this slide under low power, draw what you can see and determine which thread is on top.

_____

**Student Page –
Observing Protozoa**

Name _____

Date _____

DESCRIPTION: In the space below, draw the protozoan, (paramecium or ameba), that you observed. Draw it as it appears under low power.

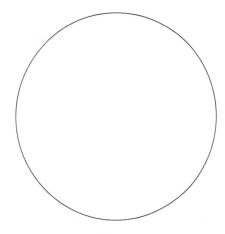

QUESTIONS:

1. In what way is this cell different from other cells you have observed?

   _____

   _____

2. What organelles were you able to identify?

   _____

   _____

3. Is this cell more or less complex than the onionskin or cheek cell? Explain your answer

   _____

   _____

4. Which life functions did you observe this organism perform?

   _____

   _____

5. How does this organism move?

   _____

   _____

Student Page –
The Role of the Cell Membrane

Name _____

Date _____

DESCRIPTION: Describe the volunteer's finger after it was removed from each beaker.

Hypertonic

_____

Isotonic

_____

Hypotonic

_____

QUESTIONS:

1. Explain the appearance of the finger after it was removed from the hypertonic solution (solution with NaCl).

    _____

    _____

2. Explain the appearance of the finger after it was removed from the isotonic solution (saline solution).

    _____

    _____

3. Explain the appearance of the finger after it was removed from the hypotonic solution.

    _____

    _____

4. What is saline solution?

    _____

    _____

5. Why is distilled water considered a hypotonic solution?

    _____

    _____

Student Page –
Selective Permeability

Name _____

Date _____

DESCRIPTION: Using the door to your classroom, your teacher has shown how an opening can be selectively permeable. In your own words, describe this demonstration.

_____

_____

_____

_____

_____

_____

_____

QUESTIONS:

1. How did the door regulate who entered or left the room?

   _____

   _____

2. How might this serve as a model for the cell membrane?

   _____

   _____

3. What is the meaning of the term selectively permeable?

   _____

   _____

4. List substances that pass through a cell membrane.

   _____

   _____

5. List substances that do not pass through a cell membrane.

   _____

   _____

Observation of an Onion Skin   Name _____

                                         Date _____

INTRODUCTION: In this activity we will prepare a slide of onion skin cells and look at them under the microscope.

EQUIPMENT AND MATERIALS:

Microscope   Slide
Piece of onion   Cover slip
Forceps   Light source
Dropper bottle with water   Lens paper
Lugol's solution

PROCEDURE:

1. When instructed by your teacher, pick up your microscope and other equipment.

2. Prepare the microscope for use as described in the activity *Observation of the Letter e.*

3. Using lens paper, clean your slide and cover slip.

4. Place two drops of water in the center of the slide and put the slide aside.

5. Using the forceps, peel the onionskin from the concave side of the piece of onion (see Diagram 2–1).

6. Place the onion skin on the drop of water on your slide. Be sure that the onion skin is not wrinkled or folded over itself.

7. Carefully cover the onion skin with a cover slip. Apply the cover slip on an angle so that you don't trap air bubbles under it (see Diagram 2–2).

8. Place your slide on the stage of the microscope, and focus it under low power. (Make sure that your microscope stage is not tilted.)

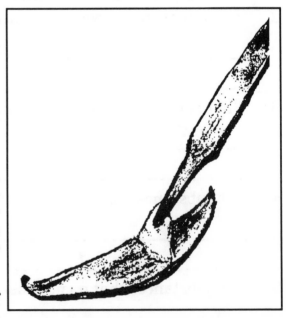

Diagram 2-1 *Removing the onionskin from a piece of onion*

9. Make a drawing of one or two onion skin cells. You cannot see all parts of the cell at the same time. If you use the fine–adjustment knob, you will be able to focus on different parts of the cell at different times. When you draw the cell, show all of the structures that you can see. Label your drawing.

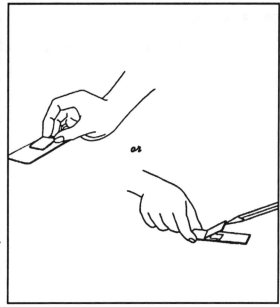

10. Remove the slide from the stage. Place a drop or two of Lugol's solution on the slide next to the cover slip. Using a small piece of paper towel, draw the stain under the cover slip so that it stains the onion skin (see Diagram 2–3).

Diagram 2-2 *Lowering the cover slip*

11. Place the slide back on the stage of the microscope, and refocus under low power. How does the stained slide look compared with the unstained slide? Can you see more structures?

12. Switch to high power, and focus with the fine adjustment.

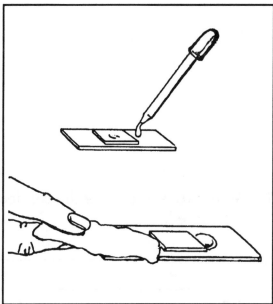

13. Make a drawing of one stained cell under high power. Label your drawing.

14. When you have completed the exercise, remove the slide, clean it as instructed by your teacher, and return it and the micro- scope to its proper place.

Diagram 2-3 *Staining the onionskin*

OBSERVATIONS:

Draw one or two unstained onion skin cells.

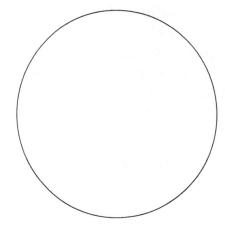

Draw a stained onion skin cell under high power.

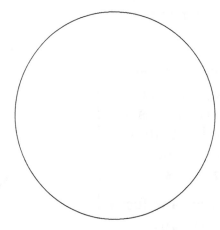

1. What are some ways the cell looks different under low power after it is stained.

    _____

    _____

2. Which structures are more visible when the cell is stained?

    _____

    _____

3. How does the cell look different under high power than under low power?

    _____

    _____

QUESTIONS:

1. Why should you lower the cover slip on an angle?

    _____

    _____

2. What is the advantage of staining a specimen?

    _____

    _____

3. Is the onionskin cell able to carry on photosynthesis? Why?

    _____

    _____

4. How does the onion skin cell, as seen under the microscope, compare with the diagrams of cells in your textbook?

    _____

    _____

5. Why do you use the fine–adjustment knob when you look at a cell under the microscope.

    _____

    _____

6. Does your diagram look exactly like the cell you saw under the microscope? Why not?

    _____

    _____

SUGGESTIONS FOR FURTHER STUDY:

- Count the number of onion skin cells across the width of the low–power field.
- Count the number of onion skin cells across the width of the high–power field.
- What is the ratio of cells under low power to cells under high power?

Observation of Human Cheek Cells

Name _____

Date _____

INTRODUCTION: In this activity you will look at animal cells to see how they differ from plant cells.

EQUIPMENT AND MATERIALS:

> Prepared slide of cheek cells
> Microscope
> Light source
> Lens paper

PROCEDURE:

1. When instructed by your teacher, pick up your microscope and prepared slide.

2. Prepare the microscope for use as described in the activity *Observation of the Letter e.*

3. Clean the slide with lens paper.

3. Place your slide on the stage of the microscope. Make sure the specimen is centered over the opening in the stage.

4. Focus the specimen under low power. If you do not see clearly focused cells, use the diaphragm to adjust the light.

5. Draw several cells as they appear under low power. Label your diagram.

6. Switch to high power, and focus with the fine–adjustment knob. You may have to use the diaphragm to increase the light. Why does the specimen seem darker under high power?

7. Make a drawing of one cell under high power. Label your diagram.

8. When you have completed the exercise, remove the slide, and return it and the microscope as instructed by your teacher.

OBSERVATIONS:

Draw several cheek cells under low power.

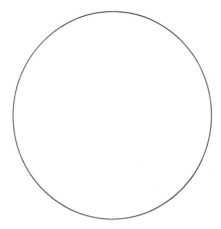

Draw one cheek cell under high power.

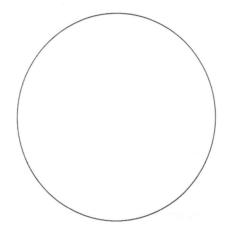

1. Why does the specimen seem darker under high power?

    _____

    _____

2. How does this cell appear different from the onionskin cell you looked at in the activity *Observation of an Onion Skin*?

    _____

    _____

3. How is this cell adapted for its function?

    _____

    _____

QUESTIONS:

1. Why did you clean the prepared slide before using it?

    _____

    _____

2. What are the functions that this cell performs?

    _____

    _____

3. How does a prepared slide differ from a wet mount such as the one you prepared in the activity *Observation of an Onion Skin*?

    _____

    _____

4. Which cell organelles were visible in this specimen?

    _____

    _____

5. What is the function of each organelle you listed in Question 4?

    _____

    _____

    _____

SUGGESTIONS FOR FURTHER STUDY:

- Look at a slide of frog skin cells. How do these cells compare with the human cheek cells?

Observation of *Elodea* Cells

Name _____

Date _____

INTRODUCTION: In this activity you will observe cells from a green plant. Because you are looking at cells in a leaf, which is made up of more than one layer, you will have to use the fine–adjustment knob to focus through the layers.

EQUIPMENT AND MATERIALS:

Microscope   Slide
Elodea leaf   Cover slip
Forceps   Light source
Dropper bottle with water   Lens paper

PROCEDURE:

1. When instructed by your teacher, pick up your microscope and other equipment.

2. Prepare the microscope for use as described in the activity *Observation of the Letter e.*

3. Using lens paper, clean your slide and cover slip.

4. Place two drops of water in the center of your slide, and put the slide aside.

5. Obtain a young leaf from the top of the plant.

6. Place the leaf on the drop of water on your slide. Be sure that the leaf is flat on the slide.

7. Carefully cover the leaf with a cover slip. Remember to avoid catching air bubbles under the cover slip.

8. Place your slide on the stage of the microscope, and focus it under low power. Make sure that the stage of your microscope is not tilted.

9. This specimen is different from the other ones we have looked at. It is more than one cell thick. You will have to use the fine–adjustment knob to focus on one cell at a time. (Remember to turn the fine–adjustment knob no more than a half turn in either direction.)

10. Choose a cell near the edge of the leaf. Draw the cell under low power. Do you see any movement in the cell? Label your drawing.

11. Switch to high power, and focus using the fine–adjustment knob. If the field is dark, use the microscope's diaphragm to increase the illumination of the field.

12. Make a drawing of one cell under high power. Remember that you cannot see all parts of the cell at the same time, but must move through the cell with fine adjustment. Label your diagram.

13. When you have completed this exercise, remove the slide, clean it as instructed by your teacher. When instructed by your teacher, return it and your microscope to its proper place.

OBSERVATIONS:

Draw one *Elodea* cell under low power.

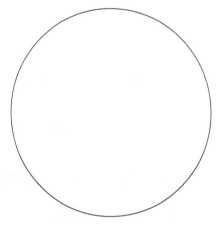

Draw one *Elodea* cell under high power.

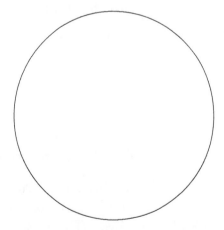

1. Were you able to see movement in the cell? If you did, describe it.

_____

_____

2. How is this specimen different from the onion skin?

    _____

    _____

3. What special problems did you encounter in looking at the *Elodea* leaf? How did you solve them?

    _____

    _____

4. Why shouldn't you use the microscope in a tilted position?

    _____

    _____

QUESTIONS:

1. What organelles were present in this cell that were not present in the onion skin cell?

    _____

    _____

2. What is this cell able to do that the onion skin cell can't do?

    _____

    _____

3. When the cytoplasm of the cell moves, the process is called *cyclosis*. Why do you think this occurs?

    _____

    _____

4. Was this cell alive or dead? Justify your answer.

    _____

    _____

5. How does this cell differ from the cheek cell?

    _____

    _____

6. How do you focus on a cell that is part of a multilayered specimen?

    _____

    _____

7. Why is it important to clean the lenses before using the microscope?

    _____

    _____

8. How would you describe the chloroplasts?

    _____

    _____

SUGGESTIONS FOR FURTHER STUDY:

- Place a plastic ruler on the stage of the microscope. What is the size of the field under low power? Estimate the width of an *Elodea* cell.

**Student Page –
The Lamb Shank**

Name _____

Date _____

DESCRIPTION: Your teacher has dissected the lamb shank for you.

1. List the different types of tissues you were able to see.

    _____

    _____

2. How were the muscles attached to the bones?

    _____

    _____

3. Describe the appearance of muscle cells.

    _____

    _____

QUESTIONS:

1. For each type of tissue you observed, list its function or functions in
    the body.

    _____

    _____

2. How are the cells that make up these tissues specialized to perform
    their functions?

    _____

    _____

3. Can you identify any cells that you think are present in the leg of a
    lamb, but that you did not observe? List them.

    _____

    _____

Student Page –
The Human Torso

Name _____

Date _____

DESCRIPTION:

Label the organs on the illustrations below, which represent the human torso.

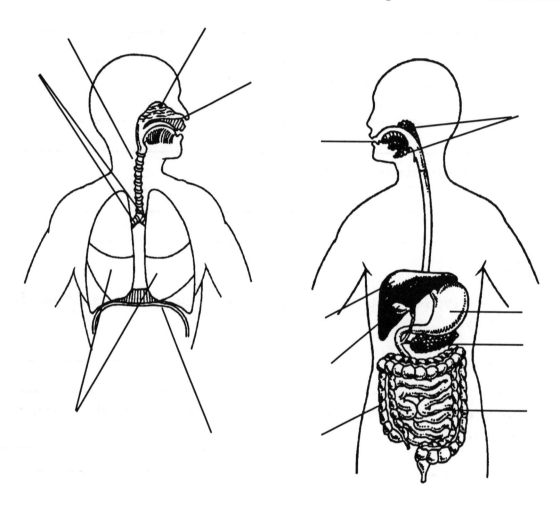

QUESTIONS:

1. (a) List each system of the body you can identify.

   _____

   (b) For each system, list the organs, from the diagram, that belong to it.

   _____

   _____

   _____

   _____

   _____

2. Which organs are found in the abdominal cavity?

   _____

   _____

3. Which organs are found in the chest cavity?

   _____

   _____

4. How can you explain the use of the term "heartburn" to describe an upset stomach?

   _____

   _____

Observation of Various Tissues

Name _____

Date _____

INTRODUCTION: In a complex organism like the human, cells have become adapted to perform special functions. Similar specialized cells are grouped into tissues. In this activity you will look at cells from a variety of human tissues to see if you can determine what each one is specialized for.

EQUIPMENT AND MATERIALS:

> Compound microscope
> Light source
> Lens paper
> Prepared slides provided by your teacher.

PROCEDURE:

1. When instructed by your teacher, pick up your microscope and other equipment.

2. Prepare the microscope for use as described in the activity *Observation of the Letter e*

3. Before using it, clean the slide with lens paper.

3. Place the first prepared slide on the stage of the microscope. Make sure that the specimen is centered over the opening in the stage.

4. Focus the specimen under low power. Note any differences you see from other cells you have looked at.

5. Make a drawing of the cell under low power. Label your diagram and write a brief description of it.

6. Repeat steps 3–5 for each slide that your teacher instructs you to look at. Make sure to clean each slide before you use it.

OBSERVATIONS:

Draw each of the cells you observed. Label each drawing.

For each of the cells you observed, write a brief description and tell how the cell is adapted for its particular function.

_____

_____

_____

_____

_____

_____

_____

_____

_____

_____

_____

_____

QUESTIONS:

1. How is a nerve cell adapted for its function?

    _____

    _____

2. Where in the body would you expect to find ciliated epithelial cells?

    _____

    _____

3. In what way are red blood cells different from other cells you looked at?

    _____

    _____

4. In what way do smooth and striated muscle cells appear different?

    _____

    _____

5. Why are red blood cells and white blood cells considered part of the same tissue?

    _____

    _____

SUGGESTIONS FOR FURTHER STUDY:

- If time permits, look at and draw additional slides of tissues that your teacher will provide.

Student Page –
Tests for Carbohydrates

Name _____

Date _____

DESCRIPTION:

a. Describe the test for starch that your teacher demonstrated.

    _____

    _____

b. Describe the test (or tests) for the presence of sugars that your teacher
    demonstrated.

    _____

    _____

QUESTIONS:

1. What is meant by the terms *positive* and *negative* when they are
    applied to food tests?

    _____

    _____

2. Describe the procedures your teacher used to light the Bunsen
    burner.

    _____

    _____

3. Which foods contain a lot of starch?

    _____

    _____

4. List three examples of sugars.

    _____

    _____

Student Page –
Tests for Protein

Name _____

Date _____

DESCRIPTION:

Describe the test (or tests) your teacher performed to test for the presence of protein in food.

_____

_____

_____

_____

_____

_____

QUESTIONS:

1. Which substances did your teacher test for the presence of protein?

   _____

   _____

2. Which foods are rich in protein?

   _____

   _____

   _____

3. If a person does not eat meat what could he eat to include protein in his diet?

   _____

   _____

4. Why does your body need proteins?

   _____

   _____

Student Page –
The Test for Fats and Oils

Name _____

Date _____

DESCRIPTION: Describe the test (or tests) for fats and oils that your teacher demonstrated.

_____

_____

_____

_____

_____

_____

QUESTIONS:

1. Can you explain the appearance of paper that has been used to **wrap** fried foods?

   _____

   _____

2. Which foods contain large amounts of fat?

   _____

   _____

3. Why is it unhealthy to eat large amounts of animal fat?

   _____

   _____

4. Before the use of electric lights, whale oil made from blubber was used as a fuel in lamps. Why was animal fat used for this purpose?

   _____

   _____

Student Page –
The Test for Vitamin C

Name _____

Date _____

DESCRIPTION: Describe the test your teacher demonstrated, for the presence
of vitamin C.

_____

_____

_____

_____

_____

QUESTIONs:

1. Which fruits and vegetables have a high vitamin C content?

_____

_____

_____

2. Can you see a problem with using indophenol to test for the presence
   of vitamin C in grape juice or other colored fruit drinks?

_____

_____

3. It takes more drops of drink A to change the color of indophenol than
   drops of drink B to cause the same color change. Which drink contains
   more vitamin C?

_____

4. Which disease is associated with a deficiency of vitamin C?

_____

**Student Page – The Extraction
of Iron From Enriched Cereal**

Name _____

Date _____

DESCRIPTION: Describe the procedure your teacher used to remove iron from the dry cereal.

_____

_____

_____

_____

_____

Which cereal did your teacher use?

_____

QUESTIONS:

1. What is meant by an enriched cereal?

_____

_____

2. How do you know that iron was present in the cereal?

_____

_____

3. Why do you need iron in your diet?

_____

_____

4. Which foods naturally contain iron?

_____

**Student Page –
Removing Calcium From Bone**

Name _____

Date _____

DESCRIPTION:

1. Describe this demonstration to remove calcium from the chicken bone.

    _____

    _____

    _____

    _____

2. Describe the result of removing calcium from the bone.

    _____

    _____

QUESTIONS:

1. Which foods contain calcium?

    _____

    _____

2. What happens to people who do not get enough calcium in their diets?

    _____

    _____

3. Why is it particularly important for pregnant women to have calcium in their diets?

    _____

    _____

4. Where in your body do you use calcium?

    _____

    _____

Student Page – The Water   Name _____
Content of Fruits and Vegetables Date _____

DESCRIPTION:

1. Describe the procedure your teacher used to determine the weight of water in the sample.

    _____

    _____

    _____

    _____

2. Record the following data from this demonstration.

    A. Weight of fruit + plastic bag = _____ g

    B. Weight of plastic bag = _____ g

    C. Weight of fruit at start (B – A) = _____ g

    D. Weight of dried fruit + plastic bag = _____ g

    E. Weight of plastic bag = _____ g

    F. Weight of dried fruit (D – E) = _____ g

    G. Weight of water in the fruit (C – F) = _____ g

3. Calculate the percentage by weight of water in the sample.

    (G ÷ C) X 100 = % water in sample

Student Page –
Nitrogen in Food

Name _____

Date _____

DESCRIPTION: Describe the test for the presence of nitrogen in food.

_____

_____

_____

_____

_____

_____

QUESTIONS:

1. What is the purpose of the red litmus paper?

_____

_____

2. What does the presence of the odor of ammonia indicate?

_____

_____

3. Why does a baby's diaper often smell of ammonia?

_____

_____

4. Which foods are high in protein?

_____

_____

5. Why must nitrogen be included in plant foods and fertilizers?

_____

_____

Student Page –
The Calorimeter

Name _____

Date _____

DESCRIPTION:

1. Label the diagram below.

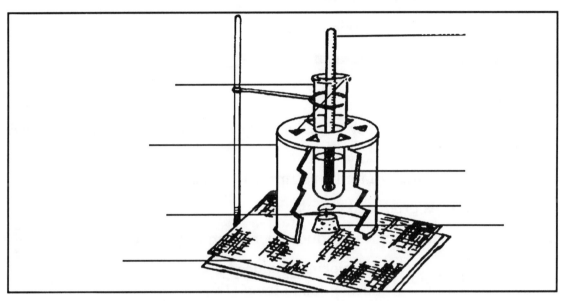

Diagram 3 - 1

2. Describe how your teacher used this equipment.

    _____

    _____

3. Record the following data.

    A. Mass of food + weighing paper = _____ g

    B. Mass of weighing paper = _____ g

    C. Mass of food (A – B) = _____ g

    D. Mass of test tube + water = _____ g

    E. Mass of empty test tube = _____ g

    F. Mass of water (D – E) = _____ g

    G. Mass of water in kg (f ÷1000) = _____ kg

H. Mass of food residue + weighing paper = _____ g

I. Mass of weighing paper = _____ g

J. Mass of food residue (H – I)= _____ g

K. Mass of food burned (C – J) = _____ g

L. Final temperature of water = _____ °C

M. Initial temperature of water = _____ °C

N. Change in temperature (L – M) = _____ °C

CALCULATIONS:

1. Calculate the number of calories produced by burning the food sample.

   Calories = change in temperature (N) X mass of water in kg (G)

   Calories produced = _____ Cal.

2. Calculate the Calories produced per gram of food burned.

$$\text{Cal./gram} = \frac{\text{Calories produced}}{\text{mass of food burned (K)}}$$

   Burning the food sample produced _____ Cal./g

QUESTIONS:

1. How might you modify this calorimeter to make it more efficient?

   _____

   _____

2. What do calories have to do with diet?

   _____

   _____

3. Which nutrients are highest in calories?

   _____

   _____

4. Why did you change the mass of water to kilograms?

   _____

   _____

Student Page –
Caloric Intake

Name _____

Date _____

In this activity you will make a list of all of the food you eat for one day. Using a calorie chart, you will list the number of calories next to each food item you have eaten. By adding all of the caloric content of all of the food you have eaten, you will calculate your caloric intake.

MEAL	DESCRIPTION AND QUANTITY OF WHAT I ATE	CALORIES
Breakfast		
Lunch		
Dinner		
Snacks		
Total Calories		

Testing the Vitamin C Content of Various Fruit Drinks

Name _____

Date _____

INTRODUCTION: Vitamin C is an important part of your diet. You may take vitamin pills that contain vitamin C, or you may drink orange juice or other fruit juices for their vitamin C content. Today we are going to test a variety of fruit drinks to see how much vitamin C each contains. To do this you will add the fruit drink, one drop at a time, to indophenol. Indophenol is a chemical that will change from blue through pink to colorless if vitamin C is added to it. Such a chemical is called an *indicator*, because it indicates, or shows, a chemical change by changing color. The more fruit drink you must add to the indophenol to get it to change color, the less vitamin C that fruit drink contains. Before you begin this activity, predict which fruit drink you think contains the most vitamin C. You will find out if you are correct when you complete this activity.

EQUIPMENT AND MATERIALS:

Indophenol   Two 10 mL graduated
Distilled water   cylinders
Ten test tubes   Eyedropper
Five samples of fruit drink in beakers   White paper
                                                Labels

PROCEDURE:

1. Using the graduated cylinder, measure 10 mL of water, and pour it into a test tube. Be sure to read the volume at the bottom of the meniscus. This is your control; label this test tube C.

2. Using the graduated cylinder, measure 10 mL of indophenol, and pour it into a test tube. This is your first test sample. Label this test tube A. Be sure to use one graduated cylinder to measure the volume of the water, and one to measure the volume of the indophenol.

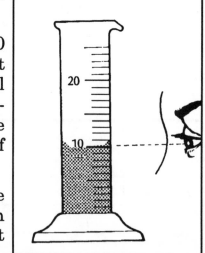

3. Using the eyedropper, add one drop of the first fruit drink to the indophenol solution in test tube A, and one drop of the fruit drink to the control (water). After the addition of each drop, shake each test tube to

Diagram 3-2 *Read volume at the bottom of the meniscus*

ensure mixing. Continue adding fruit drink, one drop at a time, to each of the test tubes until the color in each test tube is the same. Count the of number drops you added to the indophenol to change its color. Be sure to **shake** the test tube after each drop is added. If you place a white piece of paper behind the test tubes, it is easier to see the color change.

4. In the data table, record each test sample and the number of drops you added to produce the color change.

5. Repeat step 3 with each sample you are to test. Use a different eyedropper for each sample. Be sure to label each control test tube with a C, and label each test sample with a different number. Record your results in the data table.

6. When you have finished testing all of your samples, rank them, with #1 indicating the greatest concentration of vitamin C.

7. When you have completed this activity, wash all of your test tubes and graduated cylinders, and return your equipment, as instructed by your teacher.

OBSERVATIONS:

DATA TABLE		
Test Beverage	Number of drops it took for the indophenol to lose its color	Rank the test samples (#1 most vit. C)

QUESTIONS:

1. Why is it important to measure the volumes of liquid with the graduated cylinder?

    _____

    _____

2. Why did we use a test tube containing water as a control in this experiment?

    _____

    _____

3. How would you define an indicator? Have you come across any other indicators? Name them.

    _____

    _____

4. How did the vitamin C contents of these fruit drinks compare with what you thought about them before doing the experiment?

    _____

    _____

5. Describe the proper way to read a graduated cylinder.

    _____

    _____

6. What is the advantage of placing a piece of white paper behind the test tubes?

    _____

    _____

SUGGESTIONS FOR FURTHER STUDY:

- Test additional fruit drinks for their vitamin C content.

Analyzing the Data From the Activity
Testing the Vitamin C Content of
Various Fruit Drinks

Name _____

Date _____

INTRODUCTION: Making observations and collecting data are important activities of scientists. Analyzing the data is also an important task. One way of interpreting data is to put the data into the form of a graph. A graph is a helpful way to look at data and see correlations between the data. In this activity we will construct a bar graph to represent the class data from the activity *Testing the Vitamin C Content of Various Fruit Drinks.*

EQUIPMENT AND MATERIALS:

Data from the activity *Testing the Vitamin C Content*
    of Various Fruit Drinks
Graph sheet
Pencil
Calculator

PROCEDURE:

1. Your teacher will help you collect the pieces of data from the activity so that you can pool the class data. Record the class data in the data table.

2. Using a calculator, find the class average for the number of drops of each fruit drink needed to change the color of the indophenol. To find the class average for a fruit drink, you must add up all of the individual numbers of drops and divide this number by the number of students who reported data. Record the class averages in the data table.

3. Fill in the names of the fruit drinks, at the base of each column, on your graph sheet.

4. For each fruit drink, color in the column up to the number of drops required to change the color of the indophenol.

CLASS DATA TABLE ONE				
Drops Added To				
Test Beverage 1	Test Beverage 2	Test Beverage 3	Test Beverage 4	Test Beverage 5
Total				
Average				

CLASS DATA TABLE TWO	
Test Beverage	**Average number of drops it took for the indophenol to lose its color**

Vitamin C graphing sheet — fruit drinks tested

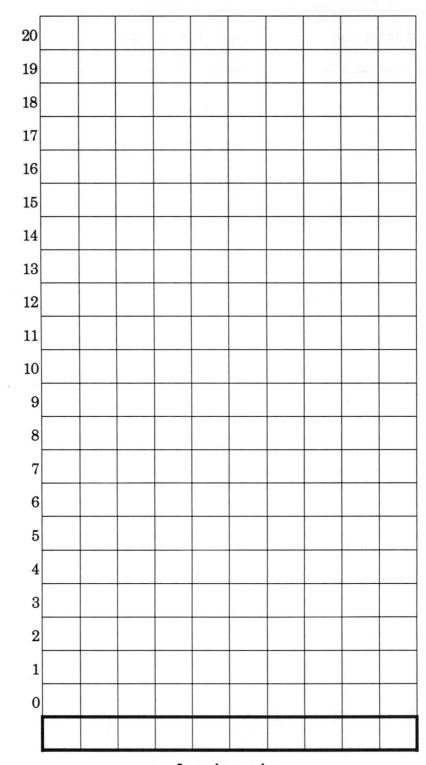

Average number of drops used

Sample number

CONCLUSIONS:

1. Which fruit drink contains the most vitamin C?

    _____

2. Which fruit drink contains the least vitamin C?

    _____

3. Which represents more vitamin C, the colored columns or the uncolored columns?

    _____

4. Rank the fruit drinks from the one containing the least vitamin C to the one containing the most.

    _____

    _____

QUESTIONS:

1. Why do we graph the class average instead of your individual results?

    _____

2. How does a bar graph make it easier to interpret the results of the experiment?

    _____

3. Can you draw any conclusions about which type of juice (canned, frozen, fresh, etc.) you should buy?

    _____

4. Where else have you seen bar graphs used?

    _____

SUGGESTIONS FOR FURTHER STUDY:

*   Design and conduct an experiment to test various vegetables for their vitamin C content.

The Caloric Content of a Peanut

Name _____

Date _____

INTRODUCTION: We have all read about Calories and are aware that they have something to do with diets and weight gain or weight loss. Whether we gain or lose weight depends upon how much energy we need and how much energy is in the food we eat. The energy content of food is measured in Calories. A Calorie is a unit of heat measurement. The device used to determine the amount of energy in food is called a calorimeter. In this activity we will use a simple calorimeter to determine how much heat energy is contained in a peanut.

EQUIPMENT AND MATERIALS:

Triple–beam balance   Water can
Weighing paper   250 mL graduated cylinder
Peanut   Stirring rod
Pin   Ring stand and ring
Matches   Wind guard

PROCEDURE:

1. Prepare the balance for use as instructed by your teacher.

2. Place a piece of weighing paper on the balance pan and find its mass. Record the mass of the weighing paper in the data table.

3. Find the mass of the peanut and record it in the data table. Remember to subtract the mass of the weighing paper.

4. Find the mass of the empty water can and record it in the data table.

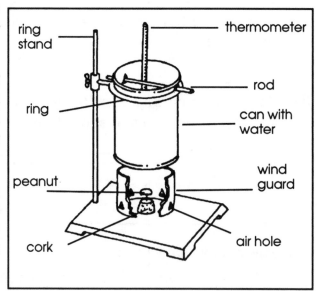

Diagram 3-3 *A simple calorimeter*

5. Using the graduated cylinder, measure 200 mL of water and add the water to the water can.

6. Find the mass of the water can with water and record it in the data table. Subtract the mass of the empty can to find the mass of the water.

7. Divide the mass of the water by 1,000 to change grams to kilograms.

8. Set up the equipment as shown in Diagram 3–4.

9. Find the temperature of the water and record it in the data table as the initial temperature.

10. Ignite the peanut, and place the wind guard over it. Lower the water can so it is close to the peanut.

11. When the peanut has stopped burning, find the temperature of the water. Record the temperature as the final temperature in the data table. Find the change in temperature.

12. Place a piece of weighing paper on the balance, and find its mass.

13. Place the remains of the peanut on the weighing paper, and find its mass. Subtract the mass of the weighing paper to find the mass of the residue. Record the mass of the residue in the data table, and find the mass of peanut burned.

DATA TABLE

A. Mass of peanut + weighing paper = _____ g

B. Mass of weighing paper = _____ g

C. Mass of peanut (A – B) = _____ g

D. Mass of can + water = _____ g

E. Mass of empty can = _____ g

F. Mass of water (D – E) = _____ g

G. Mass of water in kg (f ÷ 1000) = _____ kg

H. Mass of peanut residue
   and weighing paper = _____ g

I. Mass of weighing paper = _____ g

J. Mass of peanut residue (H – I) = _____ g

K. Mass of peanut burned (C – J) = _____ g

L. Final temperature of water = _____ °C

M. Initial temperature of water = _____ °C

N. Change in temperature (L – M) = _____ °C

CALCULATIONS

1. Calculate the number of Calories produced by burning the peanut.

   Calories = change in temperature (N) × mass of water in kg(G)

   Calories produced = _____ Calories

2. Calculate the Calories produced per gram of peanut burned.

$$\text{Cal.}/\text{gram} = \frac{\text{Calories produced}}{\text{mass of peanuts burned (K)}}$$

   Burning the peanut produced _____ Cal./g

QUESTIONS:

1. Why is it necessary to clean the pan of the balance?

   _____

   _____

2. Why do we place weighing paper on the balance?

   _____

   _____

   _____

3. Why must we always find the mass of the weighing paper or the container?

_____

_____

4. What was the purpose of the wind guard in this experiment?

_____

_____

5. Do you think our measurement of the caloric content of the peanut was very accurate? Explain why.

_____

_____

6. How could this experiment be improved?

_____

_____

7. Why was it necessary to change the mass of the water from grams to kilograms?

_____

_____

8. Why were we interested in the number of Calories produced per gram of peanut and not just the total Calories produced?

_____

_____

9. Burning a chocolate brownie produces enough heat to raise the temperature of 1 kg of water 45° C. How many Calories does the brownie contain?

_____

_____

SUGGESTIONS FOR FURTHER STUDY:
   • Test a different food for its caloric content.

Calculating Your Caloric Need

Name _____

Date _____

INTRODUCTION: Your caloric need is defined as the number of Calories of energy you need each day to operate your body. Each of us has a different caloric need. Your individual caloric need depends on such factors as your body weight, your gender, and the amount and type of activity you engage in. Today you are going to calculate the number of Calories you need to operate your body for one day.

EQUIPMENT AND MATERIALS:

Chart of energy expenditure   Calculator

PROCEDURE:

1. Using the data chart, list the activities you have engaged in during a 24–hour period. Choose one day; yesterday is probably best, because you are likely to remember it best. If you did not engage in a single activity for a whole hour, break it down into the number of minutes for each hour.

2. Using the chart, calculate the number of Calories you used for each hour of the day.

3. Add up the number of Calories you used during each hour to determine your total caloric need for one day.

DAILY CALORIES NEEDED		
Kind of Activity	**Calories needed /pound /hour**	
	Male	**Female**
Sleeping, resting	0.30	0.27
Reading, writing, eating	0.70	0.64
Light chores and study, fast typing, slow walking, class work	1.00	0.92
Concentrated study, bicycling, recreational games	2.00	1.85
Hard labor, competitive games, e. g., football, basketball, swimming	3.50	3.20

HOUR	ACTIVITIES	Wt. of student	Calories	Total for hr.
12:00–1:00				
1:00–2:00				
2:00–3:00				
3:00–4:00				
4:00–5:00				
5:00–6:00				
6:00–7:00				
7:00–8:00				
8:00–9:00				
9:00–10:00				
10:00–11:00				
11:00–12:00				

HOUR	ACTIVITIES	Wt. of student	Calories	Total for hr.
12:00–1:00				
1:00–2:00				
2:00–3:00				
3:00–4:00				
4:00–5:00				
5:00–6:00				
6:00–7:00				
7:00–8:00				
9:00–10:00				
10:00–11:00				
11:00–12:00				

Total Calories

QUESTIONS:

1. What factors affect your caloric need?

   _____

   _____

   _____

2. Do you think your caloric need is the same each day? Explain.

   _____

   _____

   _____

3. As you get older, do you expect your caloric need to change? Why?

   _____

   _____

   _____

4. What would be the result of taking in more Calories than you need?

   _____

   _____

   _____

5. What would be the result of taking in fewer Calories than you need?

   _____

   _____

   _____

SUGGESTIONS FOR FURTHER STUDY:

- Using a calorie chart, calculate your caloric intake for the same day you calculated caloric need, and compare it with your caloric need.

Student Page –
The Effects of Cooking Methods
on the Vitamin Content of Food

Name

Date

DESCRIPTION: Describe the demonstration your teacher did to show the effects of different cooking methods on the vitamin content of food.

_____

_____

_____

_____

_____

QUESTIONS:

1. How did your teacher test for the presence of vitamin C?

_____

_____

2. Which cooking method removed the most vitamin C from the food sample?

_____

_____

3. Broccoli, brussel sprouts, and string beans are good sources of vitamin C. In cooking these vegetables, what is the best method to use to preserve their vitamin C?

_____

_____

4. If you boil vegetables in water, why might it be a good idea to drink the water the vegetables were cooked in?

_____

_____

Student Page –
Chromatography of Food Dyes

Name _____

Date _____

DESCRIPTION: Describe the method your teacher used to separate the food dyes.

_____

_____

_____

_____

_____

_____

_____

_____

QUESTIONS:

1. Why are food dyes used in food?

    _____

    _____

2. Why did the food dyes separate on the paper?

    _____

    _____

3. If you wanted to do further tests on these dyes, how would this technique be useful?

    _____

    _____

4. Do you think it is a good idea to use food dyes in food?

    _____

    _____

Student Page –
Food Additives

Name _____

Date _____

Look at the label or labels you have brought to class, and list the food additives you have found them to contain. Use the list of food additives provided by your teacher to determine the function of each one.

Name of additive	Function

QUESTIONS:

1. Which of the food additives listed on your labels do you think are unnecessary? Explain your answer.

   _____

   _____

2. Which of the food additives listed on your labels do you think should be used in food? Explain your answer.

   _____

   _____

3. Why do some people insist on food with no preservatives or other additives?

   _____

   _____

   _____

**Testing the Vitamin C Content of
Orange Juice That Has Been
Treated in Various Ways**

Name _____

Date _____

INTRODUCTION: If you leave a container of orange juice out of the refrigerator all day, is the juice affected? If you keep orange juice frozen, is the juice changed? If you boil vegetables, are their vitamin contents changed? We will attempt to answer these questions today. In this activity you will perform a controlled experiment to determine the effect of boiling, freezing, and exposure to air on the vitamin C content of orange juice.

EQUIPMENT AND MATERIALS:

Four samples of juice to be tested
Four test tubes
Test tube rack
Two 10 mL graduated cylinders

Four eyedroppers
White paper
Labels
Indophenol

PROCEDURE:

1. Using the graduated cylinder to measure 10 mL of indophenol, pour 10 mL of indophenol into each of the four test tubes. Remember to read the bottom of the meniscus at eye level, with the graduated cylinder on a flat surface.

2. Label the test tubes *C, 1, 2,* and *3.*

3. Using an eyedropper, add the juice, one drop at a time, from the control to the test tube marked *C.* Shake the test tube after every drop. Continue adding the orange juice until the indophenol loses its color. Record the number of drops you added to this test tube. Place the piece of white paper behind the test tube, to help you see the color change more clearly. Because you are adding orange juice, the color of the indophenol will be slightly orange instead of colorless.

4. Using a fresh eyedropper, add the juice a drop at a time, from the beaker containing juice which has been standing to the test tube marked *1.* Shake the test tube after each drop. Continue adding this juice to test tube 1 until the indophenol loses its color. Count the number of drops you added to the indophenol, and record it in the data table.

5. Following step 4, add the orange juice that has been frozen to test tube 2 and the orange juice that has been boiled to test tube 3. Record

your data in the data table. Be sure to use a fresh eyedropper for each juice sample.

DATA TABLE	
Test tube	Number of drops for the color to change
Test tube C	
Test tube 1 (standing)	
Test tube 2 (frozen)	
Test tube 3 (boiled)	

CONCLUSION:

1. Which sample(s) showed a loss of vitamin C?

   _____

2. Which sample(s) showed no loss of vitamin C ?

   _____

3. How do your results compare to the class results?

   _____

QUESTIONS:

1. Does freezing affect the vitamin C content of orange juice?

   _____

2. Is it a good idea to leave orange juice standing exposed to the air for long periods of time? Why?

   _____

3. What effect does boiling vegetables have on their vitamin C content?

   _____

   _____

4. Why did we need a control in this experiment?

    _____

    _____

5. In what ways were the experimental samples similar to the control?

    _____

    _____

6. Why did we use a different eyedropper for each sample?

    _____

    _____

SUGGESTIONS FOR FURTHER STUDY:

-   Collect class data from this experiment. Set up a bar graph to compare the vitamin C content of juice treated in various ways.
-   Develop an experiment to test various cooking methods on the vitamin C content of various vegetables.

Student Page – The Importance
of Light in Photosynthesis

Name _____

Date _____

DESCRIPTION: Describe the demonstration performed by your teacher.

_____

_____

_____

QUESTIONS:

1. In this demonstration, what is bromothymol blue used for?

    _____

    _____

    _____

    _____

2. Why don't the contents of the test tube that is exposed to light change color?

    _____

    _____

3. What are the reactants in the process of photosynthesis?

    _____

    _____

4. From this demonstration, how do we know that plants carry on respiration?

    _____

    _____

5. Write a word equation for what occurs during photosynthesis.

    _____

    _____

**Student Page – The Need
for Light in Photosynthesis**

Name _____

Date _____

DESCRIPTION: Describe the demonstration your teacher performed to show the need for light in photosynthesis.

_____

_____

_____

_____

_____

_____

QUESTIONS:

1. What was the effect of covering part of the leaf with aluminum foil?

    _____

    _____

2. What safety precautions did your teacher take in extracting the chlorophyll from the leaf?

    _____

    _____

3. How did we determine whether photosynthesis occurred in the part of the leaf that was covered?

    _____

    _____

4. Why did we test for the presence of starch rather than the presence of glucose in the leaf?

    _____

    _____

5. What is the purpose of the Lugol's solution in this demonstration?

    _____

    _____

Student Page –
The Need for Chlorophyll

Name _____

Date _____

DESCRIPTION: Describe the demonstration your teacher performed to show the need for chlorophyll in photosynthesis.

_____

_____

_____

_____

_____

_____

_____

QUESTIONS:

1. What is a variegated leaf?

    _____

    _____

2. How did the pattern in the leaf compare with the pattern of places lacking starch?

    _____

    _____

3. What safety precautions did your teacher observe in extracting pigments from the leaf?

    _____

    _____

4. Why didn't the parts of the leaf lacking chlorophyll contain starch?

    _____

    _____

5. What solvent was used to extract the chlorophyll form the leaf?

    _____

    _____

**Student Page –
Separation of Plant
Pigments by Chromatography**

Name _____

Date _____

DESCRIPTION: Describe the technique of paper chromatography that your teacher demonstrated.

_____

_____

_____

_____

_____

_____

QUESTIONS:

1. How did your teacher transfer the plant pigments to the paper?

    _____

    _____

2. What solvent did your teacher use in this demonstration?

    _____

    _____

3. ` How many different plant pigments were found in this leaf? Name the colors of the pigments.

    _____

    _____

4. In the fall, the leaves of many plants change color. How can you account for this?

    _____

    _____

5. When you look at a leaf, why aren't all of the pigments present in a leaf visible?

    _____

    _____

Student Page –
Root Hairs

Name _____

Date _____

DESCRIPTION: Your teacher has grown radish seeds to show you the root hairs. Draw a diagram of the roots and root hairs that you have observed.

QUESTIONS:

1. What is the function of the root hairs in a plant?

   _____

   _____

2. When transplanting a plant, why must you dig beneath the roots instead of just pulling the plant out of the pot?

   _____

   _____

3. List three functions of roots.

   _____

   _____

4. What happens to a plant if its root hairs are damaged?

   _____

   _____

**Student Page –
Demonstration of Water Loss**

Name _____

Date _____

DESCRIPTION: Describe the demonstration performed by your teacher to show transpiration.

_____

_____

_____

_____

_____

_____

_____

QUESTIONS:

1. What is the purpose of the cobalt chloride paper?

    _____

    _____

2. Which surface of the leaf lost more water? Explain why.

    _____

    _____

3. How does the leaf reduce the amount of water lost by transpiration?

    _____

    _____

4. During which part of the day do you expect a plant to lose the greatest amount of water? Why?

    _____

    _____

5. What is transpiration ?

    _____

    _____

The Leaf

Name _____

Date _____

INTRODUCTION: Photosynthesis is the process by which plants change solar energy into food and release oxygen from water molecules. We, as humans, could not survive without green plants doing this. The leaf is the part of the plant in which photosynthesis occurs. The leaf has evolved to become specialized for this purpose. In this activity we will look at the leaf to see how it is adapted to perform this important function.

EQUIPMENT AND MATERIALS:

Prepared slide of the cross section of the leaf
Microscope
Light source
Lens paper

Slide
Cover slip
Dropper bottle with water
Forceps
Leaf

PROCEDURE:

Part 1: Cross–section

1. As instructed by your teacher, get your microscope and equipment.

2. Prepare the microscope for use, as you have been instructed to do.

3. Place the prepared slide of the cross–section of the leaf on the stage, and focus it under low power.

4. Draw and label the cross–section of the leaf under low power.

Part 2: Stomates

1. Place a drop of water on the slide.

2. Tear the leaf toward the main vein.

3. Using forceps pull off the thin lower epidermis.

4. Place the membrane on the drop of water, on the slide.

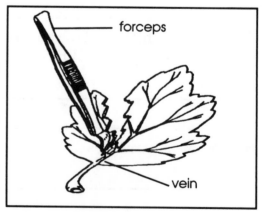

Diagram 4-1 *Removing the lower epidermis of a leaf*

5. Carefully lower the cover slip onto the specimen, on an angle so as not to trap air bubbles.

6. Place the slide on the stage, and focus on it under low power.

7. Draw and label a diagram showing an open stomate and a diagram showing a closed stomate.

8. Return your microscope and other equipment as instructed by your teacher.

OBSERVATIONS:

Part 1: Diagram of the cross–section of the leaf

Part 2: Diagrams of the stomates

Open stomate	Closed stomate

QUESTIONS:

1. In which layer of the leaf does most photosynthesis occur?

    _____

    _____

2. Why is the spongy layer built as it is?

    _____

    _____

3. In what ways does the upper epidermis protect the leaf?

    _____

    _____

4. Why are stomates located mainly on the lower epidermis?

    _____

    _____

5. How do the guard cells help to conserve water?

    _____

    _____

6. When do you expect to find the stomates open?

    _____

    _____

7. When do you expect to find the stomates closed?

    _____

    _____

SUGGESTIONS FOR FURTHER STUDY:

- Remove your slide of the lower epidermis of the leaf from the stage. Place two or three drops of salt water next to the cover slip, and draw it under the cover slip with paper toweling. Look at the slide under low power and then high power to see how the salt water affected the guard cells and the stomates.

Student Page – The Effect of Increased Surface Area

Name _____

Date _____

DESCRIPTION:

1. On the basis of this demonstration, which dissolves more quickly — granulated sugar or sugar cubes? Why is this so?

   _____

   _____

   _____

2. Which dissolves more quickly — the ground solid or the solid that is still in chunks? How can you account for this?

   _____

   _____

QUESTIONS:

1. What is the advantage of chewing food before swallowing it?

   _____

   _____

2. How does chewing food compare with grinding a solid?

   _____

   _____

3. What is the meaning of the term "surface area"?

   _____

   _____

4. Which has a greater surface area — wooden logs or wood chips?

   _____

   _____

5. Which burns faster — wood logs or wood chips? Why?

   _____

   _____

Student Page –
Mechanical Digestion

Name

Date

DESCRIPTION:

1. On the basis of this demonstration, which samples of egg white reacted most quickly with the gastric juice? How can you account for this?

2. Describe the contents of the two test tubes.

QUESTIONS:

1. Why is mechanical digestion an important part of digestion?

2. Where in your body does mechanical digestion occur?

3. What makes up gastric juice?

4. Where is gastric juice produced?

Student Page –
Hydrolysis of Starch

Name _____

Date _____

DESCRIPTION: Describe the contents and appearances of each of the two test tubes.

_____

_____

_____

_____

_____

QUESTIONS:

1. In this demonstration, which test tube was the control?

_____

_____

2. Why did the color change in the test tube that contained the enzyme?

_____

_____

3. Where in the human body does starch digestion begin?

_____

_____

4. Where in the human body is starch digestion completed?

_____

_____

5. What is the end product of starch digestion?

_____

_____

Student Page
Hydrolysis in Your Mouth

Name _____

Date _____

DESCRIPTION: Describe the taste in your mouth a few minutes after placing the cracker there.

_____

_____

_____

_____

_____

QUESTIONS:

1. How can you account for the taste change in your mouth?

   _____

   _____

2. What are some sources of starch in your diet?

   _____

   _____

3. Describe what happens to food in your mouth.

   _____

   _____

4. Define the term hydrolysis.

   _____

   _____

5. What does hydrolysis have to do with digestion?

   _____

   _____

6. Is the taste change that occurred in your mouth an example of chemical digestion or mechanical digestion? Explain your answer.

   _____

   _____

**Student Page –
Gastric Digestion**

Name _____

Date _____

DESCRIPTION: Describe the contents of each of the four test tubes.

_____

_____

_____

_____

Describe the appearance of the egg whites in each test tube, at the end of four days.

_____

_____

_____

_____

QUESTIONS:

1. Which test tubes were the controls? What was the purpose of each?

_____

_____

_____

2. Why were the test tubes placed in an incubator?

_____

_____

3. Under what special conditions does pepsin work?

_____

_____

4. Where is gastric juice produced?

_____

_____

Student Page –
Emulsification of Fats

Name _____

Date _____

DESCRIPTION: Describe the contents of each of the test tubes.

_____

_____

_____

_____

Describe what happens in each test tube after it is shaken.

_____

_____

_____

_____

QUESTIONS:

1. Which mixture took the longest to separate after being shaken? Why?

    _____

    _____

2. Define the term *emulsification.*

    _____

    _____

3. What is the function of bile in digestion?

    _____

    _____

4. Which household products act as emulsifiers? How did you determine this?

    _____

    _____

_____

Student Page –
Catalysis

Name _____

Date _____

DESCRIPTION: Describe the demonstration your teacher performed to show the function of a catalyst.

_____

_____

_____

_____

_____

QUESTIONS:

1. How did the catalyst affect the rate of this reaction?

_____

_____

2. What is the definition of a catalyst?

_____

_____

3. What is the definition of an enzyme?

_____

_____

4. Why are enzymes important to digestion?

_____

_____

5. Does a catalyst cause digestion to occur? Explain your answer.

_____

_____

**Student Page –
The Diffusion of Ammonium
Hydroxide Through a Membrane**

Name _____

Date _____

DESCRIPTION: Describe the demonstration of diffusion, performed by your teacher

_____

_____

_____

_____

QUESTIONS:

1. Why was phenolphthalein added to the test tube?

    _____

2. How can you explain the changes that occurred in the test tube?

    _____

    _____

3. At the start of the demonstration, was the concentration of ammonia greater in the test tube or in the bottle?

    _____

    _____

4. Define the term *diffusion*.

    _____

    _____

5. On the basis of this demonstration, what can you tell about the size of the ammonium hydroxide ions compared with the size of the pores in the membrane? Explain your answer.

    _____

    _____

6. How would heating the solution have affected the demonstration?

    _____

    _____

Student Page –   Name _____
Demonstration of Osmosis   Date _____

DESCRIPTION: Label the diagram of the setup
for this demonstration.

In your own words, describe what occurred
during this demonstration.

_____

_____

_____

_____

_____

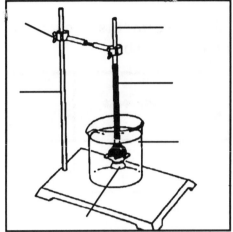

Diagram 5-1 *Demonstration of osmosis*

QUESTIONS:

1. Why did the level of the molasses in the thistle tube go up?

    _____

    _____

2. Why didn't molasses enter the beaker of water?

    _____

    _____

3. In which direction did diffusion occur — from the thistle tube to the
    beaker or from the beaker to the thistle tube?

    _____

    _____

4. Define the term *osmosis*.

    _____

    _____

**Student Page –
Osmosis in a Potato**

Name _____

Date _____

DESCRIPTION:

List the contents of each test tube, and describe what happened to the potato in each.

Tube No.	Contents	Description
1		
2		
3		

QUESTIONS:

1. Explain what happened in each of the test tubes, in terms of osmosis.

   _____

   _____

   _____

2. In which test tube is the concentration of water greater in the potato than in the test tube? Explain.

   _____

   _____

3. In which test tube is the concentration of water lower in the potato than in the test tube? Explain.

   _____

   _____

Student Page
Osmosis Through an Egg Membrane

Name _____

Date _____

DESCRIPTION: In the table below, describe the contents of each of the three beakers, and describe the changes that you observe taking place in each egg.

Beaker No.	Contents	Changes in the Egg
1		
2		
3		

QUESTIONS:

1. What happened when the colored egg was placed in distilled water? How can you account for this?

    _____

    _____

2. Why did the egg placed in water gain weight?

    _____

    _____

3. Why did the egg placed in sugar water lose weight?

    _____

    _____

The Need For Digestion   Name _____

                                           Date _____

INTRODUCTION: For nutrient molecules to be absorbed into the bloodstream, they must be small enough to pass through a membrane. Some nutrient molecules are small enough to pass through a membrane, while others are not and must be digested. Chemical digestion changes large molecules into small molecules. In this activity we will determine which nutrients must be digested. We will do this by observing which nutrients are able to diffuse through a membrane and which ones are not able to diffuse through a membrane.

EQUIPMENT AND MATERIALS:

Seven test tubes	Starch suspension
Test tube rack	Glucose solution
Test tube holder	Egg albumen
Four 250 mL beakers	Vegetable oil
Bunsen burner	Benedict's solution
Four membranes	Biuret reagent
Four rubber bands	Sudan IV
Matches	Lugol's solution
Three 10 mL graduated cylinders	Labels
Scoopula	

PROCEDURE:

1. Shake the starch suspension before using it. Half–fill one test tube with the starch suspension.

2. Cover the mouth of the test tube with a moist membrane, and secure it in place with a rubber band. Label it *starch*.

3. Half–fill the second test tube with the glucose solution.

4. Cover the mouth of this test tube with a moist membrane, and secure it in place with a rubber band. Label it *glucose*.

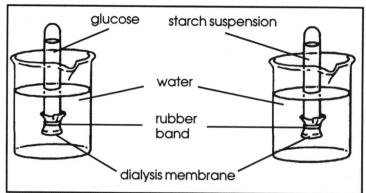

Diagram 5-2 *Appatus for this experiment*

5. Half–fill the third test tube with the albumen solution.

6. Cover the mouth of this test tube with a moist membrane, and secure it with a rubber band. Label it *protein*.

7. Half–fill the fourth test tube with oil.

8. Cover the mouth of this test tube with a moist membrane, and secure it with a rubber band. Label it *oil*.

9. Place 100 mL of water into each of the four beakers, and label them *1, 2, 3,* and *4*.

10. Into the first beaker place 10 drops of Lugol's solution, and place the test tube labeled *starch* upside down in it. Look at Diagram 5-5.

11. Into the second beaker, place the test tube labeled glucose; into the third, place the test tube labeled *protein*; and into the fourth, place the test tube labeled *oil*. Make sure that they are all upside down as in the diagram.

12. After two or three minutes, observe the test tube labeled *starch* and the beaker labeled *1*. Do you see any changes? In the data table, record any changes you observe in the test tube of starch or in the beaker.

13. After five minutes, pour into a test tube 5 mL of water from beaker *2*. Add 5 mL of Benedict's solution to the same test tube. Light the Bunsen burner as you have been instructed to do by your teacher. Heat this test tube for two minutes, and record your observations in the data table.

14. Into a test tube, pour 5 mL of the water from beaker *3*. To this test tubek add 5 mL of Biuret solution. Record your observations in the data table.

15. Into a test tube, pour 5 mL of the water from beaker *4*. Using a scoopula, transfer a few grains of Sudan IV to this test tube. Shake the test tube. Record your observations below. Add 1 mL of oil to this test tube, shake it, and record your observations. Where is the red color concentrated?

OBSERVATIONS:

STARCH (Beaker 1)

Appearance of the contents of test tube 1:

_____

_____

_____

_____

Appearance of the contents of beaker 1:

_____

_____

_____

_____

GLUCOSE (Beaker 2)

_____

_____

_____

_____

PROTEIN (Beaker 3)

_____

_____

_____

_____

OIL (Beaker 4)

_____

_____

_____

_____

CONCLUSIONS:

1. Which nutrient(s) diffused through the membrane?

    _____

    _____

2. Which nutrient(s) did not diffuse through the membrane?

    _____

    _____

3. Which of the nutrients tested must be digested?

    _____

    _____

QUESTIONS:

1. How can you explain the changes you observed in the test tube containing starch?

    _____

    _____

2. Was this a controlled experiment? Explain.

    _____

    _____

3. Why do people who need food fed to them intravenously receive glucose?

    _____

    _____

4. What are the end products of the digestion of carbohydrates, proteins and fats?

    _____

    _____

5. In the human, where does most digestion occur?

    _____

    _____

6. How is diffusion involved in absorption?

    _____

    _____

7. Is the failure to see a change considered an observation? Why?

    _____

    _____

8. How do you know that oil did not diffuse through the membrane?

    _____

    _____

SUGGESTIONS FOR FURTHER STUDY:

- Try the experiment using sausage casing in place of dialysis membranes, and compare the rate of diffusion through each.

The Deactivation of an Enzyme

Name _____

Date _____

INTRODUCTION: Have you ever wondered why hydrogen peroxide bubbles the way it does, when you put it on a cut? You are seeing the effect of an enzyme called *catalase*, an enzyme produced by your body, on the peroxide. Besides being found in brown bottles, hydrogen peroxide is produced as a waste product of metabolism and must be broken down before it can damage cells in your body. When catalase comes into contact with hydrogen peroxide, it speeds up its breakdown into water and oxygen. The bubbles we see are oxygen.

Catalase is a convenient enzyme for us to use in experiments. All enzymes are affected by heat and acids. In this activity we are going to see how heat and an acid affect this particular enzyme.

EQUIPMENT AND MATERIALS:

Three test tubes   Forceps
Test tube rack   Hydrogen peroxide
Test tube holder   Fresh liver
A 10 mL graduated cylinder   Boiled liver
Wooden splints   Acid–soaked liver
Matches

PROCEDURE:

1. Into the first test tube, place the fresh liver cube.

2. Measure 5 mL of hydrogen peroxide in the graduated cylinder, and add it to the test tube. Test the gas that is given off for the presence of oxygen, by inserting a glowing splint into the test tube. Record the results of this test and a description of your observations.

3. Into the second test tube, place a boiled liver cube.

4. Measure out and add 5 mL of hydrogen peroxide, and add it to this test tube. Record your observations below.

5. Into the third test tube, place the acid–soaked liver cube.

6. Measure out and add 5 mL of hydrogen peroxide, and add it to this test tube. Record your observations.

OBSERVATIONS:

Observation of the fresh liver

_____

_____

_____

_____

Observation of the boiled liver

_____

_____

_____

Observation of the acid–soaked liver

_____

_____

_____

_____

CONCLUSIONS:

1. Which of the three liver samples had the greatest effect on the hydrogen peroxide? Which had the least effect on the hydrogen peroxide?

_____

2. Suggest two ways that the enzyme catalase can be deactivated.

_____

_____

QUESTIONS:

1. Hydrogen peroxide is often used on cuts. On the basis of this experiment, can you explain why hydrogen peroxide is used in this way?

    _____

    _____

2. A high fever is very dangerous. On the basis of this experiment can you suggest why a fever is so dangerous? How does a high fever affect a person?

    _____

    _____

3. Are all enzymes deactivated by an acid? Can you name one that works best when an acid is present?

    _____

    _____

4. How can we determine if a gas is oxygen?

    _____

    _____

5. Can you suggest an additional experiment that can be done with catalase?

    _____

    _____

SUGGESTIONS FOR FURTHER STUDY:

-   Grind some of the liver, and add it to the hydrogen peroxide. Compare the rate at which oxygen is released with the rate at which it is released when a whole piece of liver is added to the hydrogen peroxide.

Student Page –
Taking Arterial Pulse

Name _____

Date _____

OBSERVATIONS:

In the table below, record the information requested.

CALCULATE RESTING PULSE RATE	
Fifteen–Second Intervals	Pulse Count
Interval 1	
Interval 2	
Interval 3	
Interval 4	
Interval 5	
T = Total of the five intervals	
A = Average of the intervals = T÷5	
Average for 1 minute = A x 4	

QUESTIONS:

1. Why did you find your average resting pulse in this manner?

   _____

   _____

2. Do all students have the same pulse rate? How can you account for this?

   _____

   _____

3. What does your pulse have to do with your heartbeat?

   _____

   _____

**Student Page –
Heartbeat of a Frog**

Name

Date

DESCRIPTION: In your own words, write a brief description of this demonstration.

_____

_____

_____

_____

_____

QUESTIONS:

1. What was the purpose of the Ringer's solution?

    _____

    _____

2. If the frog's heart continued to beat, would you consider the frog still alive?

    _____

    _____

3. Describe the beat of the heart.

    _____

    _____

4. What is the function of the heart?

    _____

    _____

5. What is the function of the ventricle?

    _____

    _____

**Student Page –
The Dissection Of A Heart**

Name

Date

DESCRIPTION:

1. On the diagram, label the left and right atrium, the left and right ventricles, the aorta, the veins bringing blood to the heart, the pulmonary artery and the pulmonary vein.

2. Place an *X* on every location on the diagram of the heart where valves exist.

QUESTIONS:

1. How does the thickness of the atria compare to the thickness of the ventricles? How can you account for this?

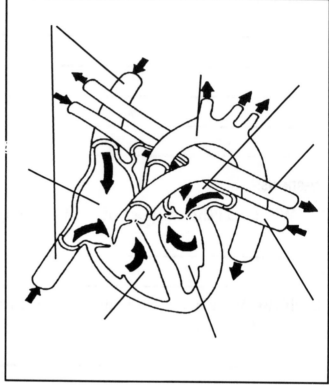

Diagram 5-3 *The heart*

2. What is the purpose of the valves?

3. Describe the appearance of the aorta.

4. Did the heart look the way you expected it to? Explain your answer.

Student Page –
Circulation in the Tail of a Goldfish

Name _____

Date _____

DESCRIPTION: In your own words, describe the circulation of blood in the tail.

_____

_____

_____

_____

_____

_____

QUESTIONS:

1. How was the fish kept alive during this demonstration?

   _____

   _____

2. Describe the blood cells you were able to see.

   _____

   _____

3. In which blood vessels were you seeing circulation occurring ?

   _____

   _____

4. How could you distinguish one kind of blood vessel from another?

   _____

   _____

5. Why didn't your teacher remove the fish's tail to demonstrate circulation?

   _____

   _____

Student Page – Oxygenated and Deoxygenated Blood

Name _____

Date _____

DESCRIPTION: Referring to the diagram, describe this demonstration.

_____

_____

_____

_____

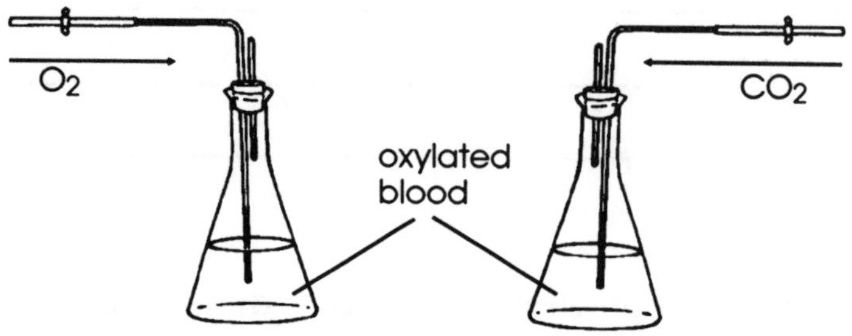

Diagram 5 - 4 *Oxygenated and deoxygenated blood*

QUESTIONS:

1. What was the purpose of adding sodium oxalate to the blood?

_____

_____

2. Describe the color of oxygenated blood.

_____

_____

3. Describe the color of deoxygenated blood.

_____

_____

4. Which blood vessel generally carry deoxygenated blood?

_____

_____

5. Why was the color of oxygenated blood different from deoxygenated blood?

    _____

    _____

6. If you cut a vein, what is the color of the blood you see. How can you account for this?

    _____

    _____

7. If a doctor or nurse draws blood from one of your veins, is it the same color as when you bleed? How can you account for this?

    _____

    _____

Student Page –
Finding Blood Pressure

Name _____

Date _____

DESCRIPTION: Describe the procedure your teacher followed in taking blood pressure.

_____

_____

_____

_____

_____

_____

QUESTIONS:

1. Why does the blood pressure reading have two numbers?

    _____

    _____

2. What is the heart doing when we record the systolic pressure?

    _____

    _____

3. What is the heart doing when we record the diastolic pressure?

    _____

    _____

4. What is the purpose of the inflatable cuff?

    _____

    _____

5. What does your teacher listen for with the stethoscope?

    _____

    _____

Student Page –
Blood Types

Name _____

Date _____

DESCRIPTION:

1. Describe the techniques your teacher used to find a person's blood type.

    _____

2. In the diagram below, draw what happened when blood typing sera were added to the blood in each part of the slide.

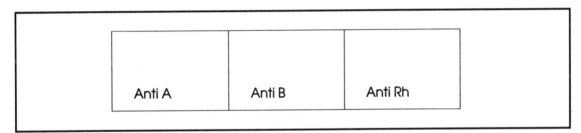

Diagram 5-5

QUESTIONS:

1. Why is it necessary to swab the finger with alcohol before taking blood?

    _____

2. In the diagrams below, show the results you would observe if a person's blood were each of the following types:

3. Why is it important to know a person's blood type?

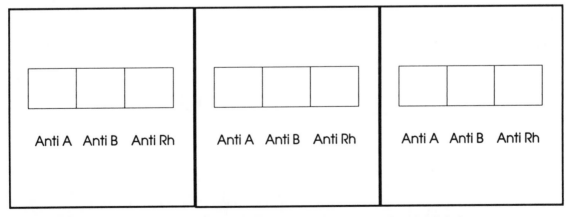

Diagram 5-8 B+   **Diagram 5-7** AB–   **Diagram 5-6** O+

4. What do the "+" and "−" indicate after the letters in the blood type?

Blood Cells

Name _____

Date _____

INTRODUCTION: When we look at blood we see a red liquid; however, blood under the microscope appears very different. In this activity we will look at a blood smear under the microscope to see the different kinds of cells that are part of our blood.

EQUIPMENT AND MATERIALS:

Prepared blood smear   Light source
Microscope   Lens paper

PROCEDURE:

1. Prepare your microscope for use, as you have been instructed by your teacher.

2. Place the slide on the microscope stage, and focus it under low power.

3. Describe what you see under observation #1, below. Do you see more than one kind of cell?

4. Look for a white blood cell; it is much larger than the red blood cells. When you have found one, describe it under observation #2, below.

5. Switch to high power, and focus with the fine–adjustment knob. (Remember **NOT** to use the coarse–adjustment knob with the high–power objective.)

6. Count the number of red blood cells in the field of vision, and record the number under observation #3, below.

7. Count the number of white blood cells in the field of vision, and record the number under observation #4, below.

8. Draw a red blood cell in the space below. Remember to label the drawing and the magnification.

9. Draw a white blood cell in the space below. Remember to label the drawing and the magnification

10. Locate some platelets in your field of vision, and draw them in the space below. If you don't see any, switch to low power, and look for a cluster on your slide. When you have found them, switch to high power, and draw them. Remember to label the drawing and magnification.

11. Return the microscope and slide, as you have been instructed by your teacher.

OBSERVATIONS:

1. Describe the blood smear under low power.

_____

_____

_____

_____

2. Describe a white blood cell.

_____

_____

_____

3. Number of red blood cells

_____

4. Number of white blood cells

_____

Draw a red blood cell   Draw a white blood cell   Draw a platelet

QUESTIONS:

1. Which blood cells are most numerous?

    _____

    _____

2. Which blood cells have nuclei, and which ones do not?

    _____

    _____

3. Do all white blood cells look alike? How do they seem different?

    _____

    _____

4. In the chart below, compare the red blood cell and the white blood cell as to shape, size, relative frequency, appearance, and function.

CELL	SHAPE	SIZE	FREQUENCY	APPEARANCE	FUNCTION

5. How do platelets compare with the red and white blood cells?

    _____

    _____

6. What is the function of a platelet?

    _____

    _____

7. Why does blood appear red?

    _____

    _____

SUGGESTIONS FOR FURTHER STUDY:

*   Look at several different blood smears, and count the number of red and white blood cells in your field of vision. How does blood count vary from one specimen to another? How can you account for these differences?

Exercise and Arterial Pulse

Name _____

Date _____

INTRODUCTION: When you are sleeping, your heart slows down; when you are running, your heart speeds up. In this activity you will find out what causes our heart to beat at different rates, at different times. Because you can't see your heart you are going to use your pulse as an indication of your heartbeat. Each time your heart beats, you will feel a pulse in one of your arteries. In this activity you will learn to take your pulse and to use it to see how exercise affects your heartbeat.

EQUIPMENT AND MATERIALS:

Watch with a second hand

PROCEDURE:

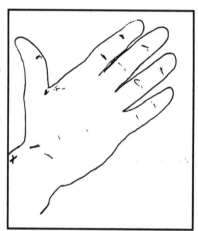

1. Place the index and middle finger of one hand about 3–4 cm above your wrist, directly behind the thumb on your other hand. Feel for your pulse.

2. Looking at your watch, count your pulse for 15 seconds and record it in the table below.

3. Repeat step 2 four times so that you have counted your pulse five times and have recorded it in the table.

4. Find your average resting pulse for 15 seconds by adding up the five 15–second pulses and dividing the total by 5.

Diagram 5-9 *Finding your pulse*

5. Multiply the average pulse you have just found by 4 to find your average pulse for one minute. Do this calculation in the table, and record your average resting pulse.

6. Using the method described in steps 1–5, find the average resting pulse of another student, and have that student find your average resting pulse. In the table below, record your average resting pulse as found by another student. See if it is the same as the average resting pulse you found for yourself.

7. Exercise as instructed by your teacher.

8. Following procedures 1–5, find your average pulse after exercise. Find your pulse as quickly after you have stopped exercising as possible. Be sure to record it in the table below.

9. After one minute, find you average pulse again. Has it returned to your resting pulse?

10. Repeat procedure 9 after two minutes. If your pulse has not returned to your resting pulse, keep taking your pulse at one–minute intervals until it does.

11. Your teacher will collect data for the class to permit you to compare your results with other students.

OBSERVATIONS:

1.

RESTING PULSE RATE	
Fifteen–Second Intervals	**Pulse Count**
Interval 1	
Interval 2	
Interval 3	
Interval 4	
Interval 5	
T = Total of the five intervals	
A = Average of the intervals = T÷5	
Average for 1 minute = A x 4	

2. Average resting pulse found by another student: _____beats/minute

3.

PULSE RATE AFTER EXERCISE	
Fifteen–Second Intervals	Pulse Count
Interval 1	
Interval 2	
Interval 3	
Interval 4	
Interval 5	
T = Total of the five intervals	
A = Average of the intervals = T÷5	
Average for 1 minute = A x 4	

4.

PULSE ONE MINUTE AFTER EXERCISE	
Fifteen–Second Intervals	Pulse Count
Interval 1	
Interval 2	
Interval 3	
Interval 4	
Interval 5	
T = Total of the five intervals	
A = Average of the intervals = T÷5	
Average for 1 minute = A x 4	

5.

PULSE TWO MINUTES AFTER EXERCISE	
Fifteen–Second Intervals	**Pulse Count**
Interval 1	
Interval 2	
Interval 3	
Interval 4	
Interval 5	
T = Total of the five intervals	
A = Average of the intervals = T÷5	
Average for 1 minute = A x 4	

Time to return to resting pulse after exercise = _____ minutes.

CONCLUSIONS:

1. How did your pulse as taken by yourself compare with your pulse as taken by another student?

   _____

   _____

2. How does exercise affect your pulse?

   _____

   _____

3. How long did it take for your pulse to return to your average resting pulse after exercising?

   _____

   _____

4. Do all students have the same pulse rate?

   _____

   _____

QUESTIONS:

1. Why were you instructed to find your average pulse rate for a 15–second interval rather than for just one 15–second interval?

    _____

    _____

2. Why were you instructed to find your pulse for 15 seconds and to multiply it by 4 instead of counting your pulse for one minute?

    _____

    _____

3. How can you account for students having different pulse rates?

    _____

    _____

4. How did exercise affect your pulse?

    _____

    _____

5. Why did your pulse rate change after exercising?

    _____

    _____

6. How can you account for the fact that different people take different amounts of time for their pulse rates to return to the resting pulse after exercise?

    _____

    _____

7. Explain what causes your pulse?

    _____

    _____

SUGGESTIONS FOR FURTHER STUDY:

*   Collect class data on average resting pulse for boys and for girls, time to return to resting pulse after exercising for boys and girls and for smokers and nonsmokers. Plot this data on graphs with the number of people on the x axis and the variables on the y axis.

**Student Page – Comparison of
Inhaled and Exhaled Air**

Name _____

Date _____

DESCRIPTION:

1. Describe the color of the bromothymol blue indicator in each flask.

    _____

    _____

    _____

2. How can you account for this difference?

    _____

    _____

    _____

QUESTIONS:

1. How does exhaled air differ from inhaled air?

    _____

    _____

2. Where does the carbon dioxide in exhaled air come from?

    _____

    _____

3. Why does your body need oxygen?

    _____

    _____

4. Why does carbon dioxide cause the bromothymol blue to change color?

    _____

    _____

Student Page –
A Voice–Activated Reaction

Name _____

Date _____

DESCRIPTION:

1. Describe the change in color that occurred in the flask.

    _____

    _____

2. How can you account for the observed change?

    _____

    _____

QUESTIONS:

1. When you exhale into the flask while "speaking into it," what do you
    add to the flask?

    _____

    _____

2. How does the presence of the exhaled gas help to explain the color
    change?

    _____

    _____

3. Suggest an experiment to test your explanation of the color change
    and to see if you are correct?

    _____

    _____

    _____

4. Why do you exhale carbon dioxide?

    _____

    _____

5. What is the purpose of respiration?

    _____

    _____

Student Page –   Name _____
The Mechanics Of Breathing   Date _____

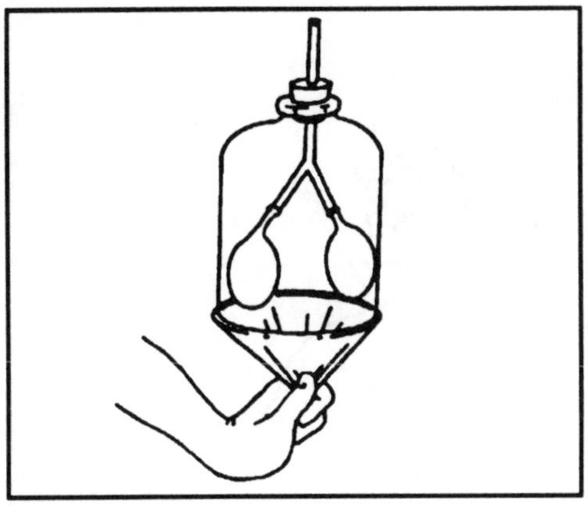

DESCRIPTION: Referring to the diagram, explain what happens when we inhale and what happens when we exhale.

_____

_____

_____

_____

_____

Diagram 5-10

QUESTIONS:

1. What is the role of the diaphragm in breathing?

_____

2. Which structure in the model represents the diaphragm?

_____

3. When a person inhales, is the pressure in his chest increased or decreased?

_____

4. What happens to your rib cage when you inhale?

_____

_____

5. What happens to your rib cage when you exhale?

_____

_____

6. Why should you breathe through your nose?

_____

_____

**Student Page –
Dissection of a Haslet**

Name _____

Date _____

DESCRIPTION:

On the diagram, label the trachea, bronchi and lungs.

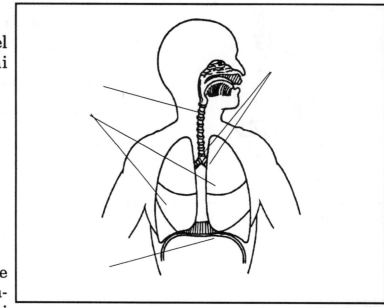

Diagram 5-11 *Human respireatory system*

QUESTIONS:

1. Describe how the anatomy of the trachea and bronchi helps them to keep their shape.

    _____

    _____

    _____

2. Describe the texture of the lungs.

    _____

    _____

3. What is the role of the epiglottis?

    _____

    _____

4. How does the respiratory system clean itself?

    _____

    _____

**Student Page –
The Spirometer**

Name _____

Date _____

DESCRIPTION:

1. Describe the structure of the spirometer.

    _____

    _____

    _____

2. Explain how the spirometer is used to find lung capacity.

    _____

    _____

    _____

QUESTIONS:

1. What is meant by lung capacity?

    _____

    _____

2. Do all people have the same lung capacity?

    _____

    _____

3. How can a person increase his lung capacity?

    _____

    _____

4. Why is it important for athletes to have large lung capacities?

    _____

    _____

5. People who live on high mountains often have large lung capacities.
    How can you account for this?

    _____

    _____

Body Changes During Breathing

Name _____

Date _____

INTRODUCTION: Respiration is the process by which we burn food to release energy. For this process to occur, our cells need oxygen. During respiration we produce carbon dioxide and water as wastes. Breathing is the process by which we bring oxygen into our bodies and get rid of the carbon dioxide and water vapor we produced as wastes. In this activity we will learn something of the process of breathing.

EQUIPMENT AND MATERIALS:

      Tape measure   Straw
      Two test tubes   Bromothymol blue or
      Test tube rack   limewater

PROCEDURE:

Part 1: Changes in your chest and abdomen

1. Place a tape measure around your chest, just below your armpits. Measure the size of your chest after you inhale normally. Record your measurement in the table under *Observations* part 1.

2. Measure your chest after you exhale normally. Record your measurement in the table below.

3. Inhale as deeply as possible, and measure your chest. Record your measurement in the table below.

4. Exhale all the air you can, and measure your chest. Record your measurement in the table below.

5. Place the tape measure around your abdomen, near your last rib. Measure the size of abdomen after you inhale normally. Record your measurement in the table below.

6. Measure your abdomen after you exhale normally. Record your measurement in the table below.

7. Inhale as deeply as possible, and measure your abdomen. Record your measurement in the table below.

8. Exhale all the air you can, and measure your abdomen. Record your measurement in the table below.

Part 2: Changes in the amount of CO_2 you produce

1. Fill each of the test tubes full of bromothymol blue. Label them *1* and *2*.

2. Using a straw, bubble your breath into test tube 1 until the color changes from blue to yellow. Record in the table below the time it takes for the bromothymol blue to change color.

3. Exercise vigorously for about five minutes, according to your teacher's directions. (If you are not in sufficiently good health, inform your teacher, and do not do this.)

4. Using a straw, bubble your breath into test tube 2 until the color of the bromothymol blue changes to yellow. Record in the table below the time it takes for the color to change.

OBSERVATIONS:

Part 1

BREATHING MEASUREMENT				
Body Area	**Inhalation**		**Exhalation**	
	Normal	**Deep**	**Normal**	**Deep**
Chest				
Abdomen				

Part 2

EXHALED CO_2	
Test Tube No.	**Time to Change the Color of Bromothymol Blue (in seconds)**
1	
2	

CONCLUSIONS:

1. When did your chest have the greatest measurement?

    _____

    _____

2. When did your chest have the smallest measurement?

    _____

    _____

3. When did your abdomen have the greatest measurement?

    _____

    _____

4. When did your abdomen have the smallest measurement?

    _____

    _____

5. How can you explain these changes?

    _____

    _____

    _____

6. When did you produce more carbon dioxide — before or after exercising?

    _____

    _____

QUESTIONS:

1. Explain the changes you noted in the size of your chest and of your abdomen in terms of what happens when you breathe.

    _____

    _____

2. People who live on high mountains, where the air is thin, often develop large chests. How can you explain this?

    _____

    _____

3. How does exercise affect the amount of carbon dioxide you exhale?

_____

_____

4. Briefly describe what happens when you inhale.

_____

_____

5. Briefly describe what happens when you exhale.

_____

_____

6. How can you explain why you breathe faster when you are running?

_____

_____

7. Heavy smokers often find that after many years of smoking their chests expand. How can you account for this?

_____

_____

SUGGESTIONS FOR FURTHER STUDY:

- Collect class data and compare the changes in chest size for boys and for girls.

Student Page –
Excretion of Water

Name _____

Date _____

DESCRIPTION:

1. Describe how your teacher demonstrated the presence of water in your breath.

    _____

    _____

2. What are you seeing when you see your breath on a cold day? Explain.

    _____

    _____

QUESTIONS:

1. When we exhale, what wastes are we excreting?

    _____

    _____

2. Why are our lungs considered organs of excretion?

    _____

    _____

3. What process in our body releases both water and carbon dioxide as wastes?

    _____

    _____

4. In addition to exhaling, how else do we excrete water?

    _____

    _____

Student Page –
Dissection of the Kidney

Name _____

Date _____

DESCRIPTION: Draw the kidney, and label the cortex and medulla.

QUESTIONS:

1. What is the principal function of the kidney?

    _____

    _____

2. How is urine transported from the kidney to the bladder?

    _____

    _____

3. Which tube removes urine from the bladder?

    _____

    _____

4. What is a kidney stone? Why is it so painful?

    _____

    _____

Student Page –
Evaporation

Name _____

Date _____

DESCRIPTION:

1. Describe this demonstration

   _____

   _____

2. Which arm feels colder? How can you account for this?

   _____

   _____

QUESTIONS:

1. How does our body regulate temperature?

   _____

2. Why is it dangerous for our body temperature to get too high?

   _____

3. When do we sweat the most?

   _____

4. What is the content of your perspiration?

   _____

5. Why is it a good idea to eat some salt on very hot days?

   _____

   _____

Student Page —
Lamb Shank Dissection

Name _____

Date _____

DESCRIPTION: Your teacher has dissected the shank of an animal. Describe what you were able to observe.

_____

_____

_____

_____

QUESTIONS:

1. What is the relationship between tendons and bones?

_____

_____

2. What is the function of a ligament?

_____

_____

3. What is the relationship between muscles and bones in locomotion?

_____

_____

4. Why is it important for an animal to be able to move from place to place?

_____

_____

5. Where in your leg do you expect to find ligaments?

_____

_____

6. Describe the symptoms of tendinitis.

_____

_____

Student Page –
Bones

Name _____

Date _____

DESCRIPTION:

1. Describe what you were able to see in the x–ray.

   _____

   _____

2. Describe the cross–section of the bone that your teacher showed you.

   _____

   _____

   _____

QUESTIONS:

1. What evidence have you seen to show that bones are made of living tissue?

   _____

   _____

2. What are the functions of the skeleton?

   _____

   _____

3. What occurs in the bone marrow?

   _____

   _____

4. Why does a doctor often put a broken leg in a cast?

   _____

   _____

**Student Page –
Chicken Feet**

Name _____

Date _____

DESCRIPTION: Describe what you were able to observe after your teacher cut open the chicken's foot.

_____

_____

_____

_____

_____

QUESTIONS:

1. What happened when your teacher pulled a tendon?

    _____

    _____

2. In a living bird, what would pull the tendons?

    _____

    _____

3. Describe a tendon.

    _____

    _____

4. Where in your leg would you expect to find tendons?

    _____

    _____

Student Page –
Moving Bones

Name _____

Date _____

DESCRIPTION:

1. Describe how your teacher attached the rubber bands to the bones.

    _____

    _____

2. What are the rubber bands meant to represent?

    _____

    _____

3. When one of the rubber bands in a pair contracted, what happened
    to the other one in the pair? Why must they work in this way?

    _____

    _____

QUESTIONS:

1. Why must muscles work in pairs?

    _____

    _____

2. What is a flexor?

    _____

    _____

3. What is an extensor?

    _____

    _____

4. What would happen if both a flexor and an extensor contracted at the
    same time?

    _____

    _____

5. What happens when a muscle contracts?

    _____

    _____

Bones, Joints and Muscles

Name _____

Date _____

INTRODUCTION: The bones of your skeleton serve several purposes including protection, support, and movement. Parts of the skeleton surround the organs to protect them from injury should you bang into something or something rub against you. Parts of your skeleton support your body, giving it its shape. Some of your bones act as levers for movement. In this activity we will look at the skeleton to determine the functions of different bones.

Joints are the places where bones come together. It is at the joints that movement can occur. Some of our joints are like a ball and socket, permitting us to twist and turn our limbs; while others are like a hinge, permitting bones to move back and forth. In this activity we will look at some of the joints of the body, to determine which kind they are.

Muscles also serve different purposes and are of three different types: striated or voluntary muscles, smooth or involuntary muscles, and cardiac muscle. Cardiac muscle is the muscle of your heart. Striated muscle makes up the muscles that you control, such as the muscles that move your arms or legs. Smooth muscle makes up the muscle you don't control such as the diaphragm or the muscles of your stomach or intestines. In this activity we will look at the three types of muscle tissue under the microscope.

EQUIPMENT AND MATERIALS:

Skeleton   Light source
Prepared slides of muscle tissue   Lens paper
Microscope

PROCEDURE:

Part 1: Bones of the skeleton

When you look at the skeleton, you will find several bones labeled with numbers. Study each bone carefully to determine its function. When you have determined its function, fill in the information about it in the table below. Remember that some bones may serve more than one purpose. Be sure to study and fill in the information for all of the bones with numbers. For each numbered bone, list the number of the bone, the function or functions of the bone, and your reason for making this determination.

Part 2: Joints

When you look at the skeleton, you will find that several of the joints are labeled with letters. Study each joint to determine which type of joint it is. You may, as directed by your teacher, move the bones to see how the joint permits movement. Be sure to study all of the joints that are labeled with a letter. Fill in the information in the chart below for each joint you studied. For each labeled joint, list the letter, the type of joint, and your reason for making this determination.

Part 3: Muscles

1. As instructed by your teacher, get your microscope and other equipment.

2. Prepare the microscope for use as you have been instructed to do.

3. Place the slide labeled *striated muscle* on the stage, and focus it under low power. On the data sheet draw the striated muscle tissue under low power. Be sure to label your drawing.

4. Place the slide labeled *smooth muscle* on the stage, and focus it under low power. On the data sheet, draw the smooth muscle tissue under low power. Be sure to label your drawing.

5. Place the slide labeled *cardiac muscle* on the stage, and focus it under low power. On the data sheet, draw the cardiac muscle tissue under low power. Be sure to label your drawing.

6. When instructed by your teacher, return the microscope and slides to their proper places.

OBSERVATIONS:

Part 1: Bones

For each of the numbered bones on the skeleton, list the number, the function or functions you think the bone performs, and the reason you think this is the function of the bone.

Bone No.	Function	Reason

Part 2: Joints

For each of the labeled joints, list the letter of the joint, the type of joint it is, and your reason for thinking this.

Joint Letter	Type	Reason

Part 3: Muscles

A. Draw striated muscle tissue.

B. Draw smooth muscle tissue.

C. Draw cardiac muscle tissue.

QUESTIONS:

1. The bones of the rib cage and the skull protect parts of the body. Which organs are protected by these bones?

    _____

    _____

    _____

2. How would you describe the bones that are involved in movement?

    _____

    _____

3. Which type of joint permits you to move your arm in a circle?

    _____

    _____

4. How would you classify the joints of your fingers and toes?

    _____

    _____

5. Why are striated muscles also called voluntary muscles?

    _____

    _____

6. Which organs in your body are made up of smooth muscle?

    _____

    _____

7. Why are the voluntary muscles called striated or striped muscles?

    _____

    _____

8. What are the functions of ligaments and tendons in movement?

    _____

    _____

9. Why are the bones of the arms and legs called levers?

    _____

    _____

SUGGESTIONS FOR FURTHER STUDY:

- Get samples of chickens' feet. Dissect them to show the presence of tendons and ligaments.

MEDICAL HISTORY

Name _____ Home phone _____

Address_____ Business phone _____

Chief
complaint _____ Onset _____ Symptoms _____

_____

_____

Frequency _____ Duration _____Other areas affected _____

Have you had this before? _____ Date of last episode _____

What treatment was given?_____

What do you think caused this to happen? _____

What changes have you had to make in your life because of this problem? _____

Have you or anyone in your family ever had the following:

	Patient	Family Member		Patient	Family Member
High blood pressure	_____	_____	Tuberculosis	_____	_____
Rheumatic fever	_____	_____	Lung cancer	_____	_____
Heart attack	_____	_____	Pneumonia	_____	_____
Heart surgery	_____	_____	Asthma	_____	_____
Varicose veins	_____	_____	Emphysema	_____	_____
Leg ulcers	_____	_____	Black outs	_____	_____
Seizures	_____	_____	Alzheimer's	_____	_____
Migraines	_____	_____	Multiple sclerosis	_____	_____
Psychiatric illness	_____	_____	Cancer (type)	_____	_____
Heart condition	_____	_____	Renal problems	_____	_____
Hemophilia	_____	_____	Anemia (type)	_____	_____
AIDS or ARC	_____	_____	Hepatitis	_____	_____
Diabetes	_____	_____	Bowel disease	_____	_____
Ulcers	_____	_____			
V. D. (type)	_____	_____			

HAVE YOU EVER HAD:

Shortness of breath _____ When?_____

Wheezing _____ Unusual sneezing _____ Cough that wont go away __

Bloody sputum _____ Pain in chest _____ Where? When?_____

An upper respiratory infection _____ How often? _____

Chest x–rays _____ When? _____

Head injury? _____ When? _____ Describe _____

Fainting or dizzy spells _____ Frequency _____ When?_____

Brain scan _____ EEG _____ Spinal tap _____

Blood transfusion _____ When?_____ Why?_____

Chemotherapy?_____ When?_____ Why? _____ What kind?_____

Exposure to radiation _____ When? _____

Bleeding gums _____ Nose _____ Rectum _____ Between periods _____

Do you bruise easily? _____

Blood tests _____ When?_____ What kinds? _____

Surgery _____ Describe_____

Right now, who is your physician? _____

What medications do you take?

Name _____ Dose_____ Frequency_____

Name_____ Dose_____ Frequency_____

Name_____ Dose_____ Frequency_____

Are you on a special diet?_____ Describe_____

Do you exercise?_____ How often?_____ What kind?_____

Do you smoke?_____ How much?_____

Do you drink alcohol?__ How much? _____

Do you use drugs?_____ What kind?_____ How often?_____

Have you lost or gained weight recently?_____

How often do you have a bowel movement?_____

Do you have diarrhea?_____ Constipation?_____

Do you have nausea? _____ Vomiting?_____ Loss of appetite?_____

Excess belching?_____ Gas?_____

Have you had menstrual problems? _____

Is there anything else you want me to know? _____

_____

Student Page –
Reading the Thermometer

Name _____

Date _____

DESCRIPTION:

1. Record your body temperature before and after exercising.

    Before:_____After:_____

2. Write the temperature indicated on the thermometers below.

QUESTIONS:

1. Why is it important to determine if a person has a fever?

    _____

    _____

2. Why can a high fever be dangerous?

    _____

    _____

3. What should you do if a person has a high fever?

    _____

    _____

4. Do all people have the same body temperature?

    _____

    _____

5. How did exercising affect your temperature?

    _____

Student Page –
Taking Pulse

Name _____

Date _____

DESCRIPTION: Describe how you find a person's pulse.

_____

_____

Record the information requested in the chart below

CALCULATE RESTING PULSE RATE	
Fifteen–Second Intervals	Pulse Count
Interval 1	
Interval 2	
Interval 3	
Interval 4	
Interval 5	
T = Total of the five intervals	
A = Average of the intervals = T÷5	
Average for 1 minute = A x 4	

QUESTIONS:

1. What information does a doctor get by taking your pulse?

_____

_____

2. In taking a person's pulse, why shouldn't you use your thumb?

_____

_____

3. How does exercising affect your pulse? Explain why this is so.

_____

_____

Student Page –
Eyes, Ears, and Throat

Name _____

Date _____

DESCRIPTION:

1.   a. Draw a diagram of the eye to show normal and abnormal dilation of the pupil.

    b. Describe the lens your teacher showed you.

    _____

    _____

    c. Describe the eye chart and its purpose.

    _____

    _____

2. Describe a normal eardrum and a diseased ear drum.

    _____

    _____

3. Describe how a diseased throat appears different form a normal throat.

    _____

    _____

    _____

    _____

QUESTIONS:

1. What may a dilated pupil indicate to the doctor?

2. What does your doctor look for when he examines your eye?

3. Why is it important to have your eyes checked regularly?

4. What is the purpose of the eardrum?

5. How may loud noises affect your eardrum?

6. Describe the symptoms of a sore throat.

7. What is the doctor looking for when he examines your throat?

Student Page –
Heart Sounds

Name _____

Date _____

DESCRIPTION: Describe the sound of a normal heartbeat and the sounds of the heartbeat of a person with a heart murmur and that of a person with an arrhythmic heartbeat.

_____

_____

_____

_____

QUESTIONS:

1. What causes the sounds we hear when we listen to a heartbeat?

_____

_____

2. What causes a heart murmur?

_____

_____

3. Does your heart beat at the same rate all the time?

_____

_____

4. What might affect your heartbeat?

_____

_____

5. In which part of your body is your heart located?

_____

_____

**Student Page –
Personal Medical History**

Name

Date

Your teacher has given you a copy of a personal medical history form that a doctor might ask you to fill out. Complete the information on the form, and answer the questions below.

QUESTIONS:

1. Why does the doctor want to know your chief complaint and information about it?

    _____

    _____

2. If you are in the doctor's office for an annual medical check–up, would you have a chief complaint?

    _____

    _____

3. Why does the doctor want information about your family?

    _____

    _____

4. What can a doctor find out from your answers to the questions under "Have you ever had "?

    _____

    _____

5. Why should your doctor know about medications you are taking?

    _____

    _____

6. Why should your doctor know about your use of drugs, alcohol, and cigarettes?

    _____

    _____

7. Why is it important for you to be truthful in filling out this form for your doctor?

_____

_____

8. Why must your doctor know about your own personal medical history?

_____

_____

9. Do you have to fill out a form like this every time you visit your doctor? Explain.

_____

_____

10. What is the meaning of the terms: *renal problems, sputum, chemotherapy, bowl, duration?*

_____

_____

_____

_____

_____

Doctor's Diagnosis

Name _____

Date _____

INTRODUCTION: When you visit your doctor, he asks you a series of questions about yourself and your family. He is taking your personal and family histories. He uses the information you provide in your answers to diagnose your illness. As part of this procedure, he reviews the systems of the body, deciding which system of your body is affected by each symptom you describe. Today you will get a chance to play the part of a doctor and decide which system is affected, by listening to the symptoms described by your patient. We will do this in the form of a game. Carefully read the directions for this game in the procedure below, and listen to your teacher's description of the game.

EQUIPMENT AND MATERIALS:

   Box of game cards

PROCEDURE:

1.   Your teacher will assign you to a team and tell you which teams are playing together. When you have been assigned, you will need one box of game cards for the two teams.

2.   Using a method described by your teacher, decide which team will be the doctors and which team will be the patients, for the first round of play.

3.   The patient team takes the box of game cards and takes out the first card.

4.   One member of the patient team will read the symptoms listed on the front of the card. On the back of the card, you will find the correct system to be identified, along with additional information to help you answer the questions that the doctor team is allowed to ask.

5.   The doctor may ask you three questions about additional symptoms — or to clarify one of the symptoms on the original card.

6.   The patient team must answer this question as accurately as possible, on the basis of the information on the card. If the doctor team thinks the information is wrong, it can challenge the patient team answer. All challenges will be decided by the teacher. If the doctors successfully challenge an answer they gain one additional point.

7. The doctor team must now name the system associated with the symptoms described. All members of the team must agree on the diagnosis. If they correctly name the system and did not ask any questions, they score five points. For every question they ask, they score one less point. The correct answer without any additional questions is worth five points. The correct answer with one question is worth four points, with two questions is worth three points, and with three questions is worth two points. If the doctor team is wrong the patient team scores one point.

8. Place the used card at the back of the box of playing cards. Give the box of cards to the other team. Now they are the patients, and you are the doctors.

9. At the end of each round, the teams switch roles and the box is transferred to the other team. The members of the patient team must take turns reading the symptoms.

10. The team with the highest score at the end of the game is the winner.

Blood Pressure and Heartbeat

Name _____

Date _____

INTRODUCTION: An important part of any visit you make to the doctor's office is having your blood pressure taken and having the doctor listen to your heart. In this activity you will get a chance to do both of these things. You will take the blood pressure of your laboratory partner and listen to his/or her heart.

EQUIPMENT AND MATERIALS:

Sphygmomanometer   Stethoscope

Procedure:

Part 1: Blood Pressure

1. Place the cuff of the sphygmomanometer snugly around the upper arm of your lab partner. The arm should be free of clothing.

2. Place the manometer dial so that it faces you.

3. Locate the brachial artery of your partner. This artery is located on the inner part of the arm, near the biceps. Feel for the pulse in this artery.

4. Keeping your fingers on the pulse point, inflate the cuff to a mark 30 mm above where you feel the pulse stop. Do not overinflate the cuff.

5. Deflate the cuff slowly and, feeling for the pulse to start, note the reading on the manometer dial.

6. Place the bell of the stethoscope over the brachial artery.

7. Inflate the cuff again to 30 mm above the reading you noted when you deflated the cuff (the reading you noted in procedure 5).

8. Deflate the cuff slowly, about 3 mm per second. Note what the reading is when you hear two consecutive beats. This is the systolic pressure. Record the systolic pressure in the data table.

9. Continue to deflate the cuff until the sounds disappear. Note the reading on the monometer dial when this happens. This is the diastolic pressure. Record the diastolic pressure in the data table.

Part 2: Heartbeat

1. Place the ear tips of the stethoscope in your ears and place the disc of the stethoscope on your partner's chest. Listen for the sound of

his/or her heart. If it does not sound loud and clear, move the disc around on the chest until the sound improves.

2. The first sound you hear (*lubb*) is the sound of the valves between the atria and ventricles closing. The second sound you hear (*dup*) is the sound made by the closing of the valves in the pulmonary artery and in the aorta.

3. Describe the sound that the heart makes. As you move the stethoscope, do the sounds get louder or softer? Write a brief description below of the sound of the heart.

OBSERVATIONS:

Part 1

Systolic Pressure   = _____ mm

Diastolic Pressure   = _____ mm

Part 2

Description of the heartbeat

_____

_____

_____

CONCLUSIONS:

1. What is the heart doing when we record the systolic pressure?

_____

_____

2. What is the heart doing when we record the diastolic pressure?

_____

_____

3. Which sound (*lubb* or *dup*) *is associated with the systole?*

_____

_____

4. Which valves close when the heart contracts?

_____

_____

QUESTIONS:

1. Define the terms *systole* and *diastole*.

    _____

    _____

2. Why does the blood pressure have two numbers?

    _____

    _____

3. What factors may affect a person's blood pressure?

    _____

    _____

4. Why did you feel for the pulse in the arm before taking pressure?

    _____

    _____

5. Trace the flow of blood through the heart.

    _____

    _____

SUGGESTIONS FOR FURTHER STUDY:

- Collect class data on people's blood pressure and compare the range of blood pressures in your class.

Student Page –　　　　　　　Name _____
Stimulus and Response　　　　　Date _____

DESCRIPTION:

1.　Describe your reaction to your teacher's behavior.

　　_____

　　_____

2.　Describe the reaction of the eye's pupil to light being shined in it.

　　_____

　　_____

QUESTIONS:

1.　In each of the demonstrations, what is the stimulus and what is the response?

　　_____

　　_____

　　_____

2.　Give three examples of stimuli and the responses that they cause.

　　_____

　　_____

　　_____

3.　For each of the stimuli described above, what is the receptor that received the stimulus?

　　_____

　　_____

　　_____

4.　For each of the responses described above, what is the effector?

　　_____

　　_____

　　_____

5.   Which parts of your body act as receptors?

_____

_____

_____

Student Page – Human Reflexes

Name _____

Date _____

DESCRIPTION:

In the space below, describe each of the reflexes you observed.

_____

_____

_____

_____

_____

_____

_____

_____

QUESTIONS:

1. Can you control a reflex? Explain.

_____

_____

2. When people learn how to drive, they often say that they have developed good reflexes. Is this an accurate description of what they have learned? Explain your answer.

_____

_____

3. How do reflexes differ from habits?

_____

_____

4. What is the difference between a reflex and an reflex arc?

_____

_____

Student Page –
Reflexes in a Frog

Name _____

Date _____

DESCRIPTION:

In the space below, describe the reflexes you observed in the frog.

_____

_____

_____

_____

_____

_____

_____

_____

QUESTIONS:

1. For each of the reflexes you observed, what is the receptor and what is the effector?

    _____

    _____

2. Describe the path of a reflex arc.

    _____

    _____

3. For each of the reflexes you observed, what is the stimulus and what is the response?

    _____

    _____

Student Page –   Name _____
The Brain   Date _____

DESCRIPTION:

1. Describe the appearance of the brain.

    _____

    _____

    _____

2. Which parts of the brain were you able to see?

    _____

    _____

QUESTIONS:

1. What is the function of the cerebrum?

    _____

    _____

2. How does the surface area of the cerebrum increase?

    _____

    _____

3. What is the function of the cerebellum?

    _____

    _____

4. What activities are controlled by the medulla?

    _____

    _____

5. In what ways is your brain different from the one you observed?

    _____

    _____

Student Page –
Neurons

Name _____

Date _____

DESCRIPTION:

Label the parts of the neuron on the diagram below.

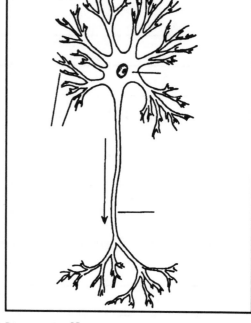

Diagram 7-1 *Neuron*

QUESTIONS:

1. How does this diagram compare with the neuron you observed?

   _____

   _____

   _____

   _____

   _____

   _____

2. Are all neurons alike?

   _____

   _____

3. How does a sensory neuron differ from a motor neuron?

   _____

   _____

4. What kinds of neurons do you think make up the brain?

   _____

   _____

5. Why do some neurons have such long axons?

   _____

   _____

Mapping Sensory Neurons

Name _____

Date _____

INTRODUCTION: When you list your sense organs, do you include your skin? Your skin is an important organ for sensing pressure, pain, heat and cold. You recognize the texture of things by using the nerve endings in your skin. Is your skin equally sensitive in all parts of your body? In this activity we are going to determine the distance between sensory neurons in different parts of your skin. We will do this by seeing how far apart two points must be for us to recognize them, by touch, as being separate.

EQUIPMENT AND MATERIALS:

> Cardboard square
> Two pins
> Metric ruler

PROCEDURE:

You will take turns performing this activity on one another. Your teacher will tell you which of you is to do the experiment first. These instructions are for the student who is performing the experiment.

1. Place one pin through the cardboard.

2. Place the second pin approximately 5 mm from the first.

3. Have the other student close his or her eyes or look away during this experiment.

4. Place the two points of the pins on the back of the subject's hand, and ask the subject if he or she feels one pin or two.

5. Move the pin a little farther apart, and ask the subject again if he or she can feel one pin or two.

6. Continue moving the pins apart (5 mm at a time), until the subject can recognize two distinct pinpoints. Measure this distance, and record it in the chart below.

7. Repeat steps 3–6 on the palm of the subject's hand, and record the measurement in the table below.

8. Repeat steps 3–6 on the inside of the subject's arm, and record the measurement in the table below.

9. Repeat steps 3–6 on the subject's leg, and record the measurement in the table below.

10. You will now become the subject, and your partner will perform the experiment.

OBSERVATIONS:

DATA TABLE

1. Back of hand _____ mm

2. Palm of hand _____ mm

3. Inside of arm _____ mm

4. Leg _____ mm

Arrange the parts of the body from most sensitive to least sensitive.

CONCLUSIONS:

1. Which part of your skin is most sensitive?

_____

2. Which part of your skin is least sensitive?

_____

QUESTIONS:

1. Why do you think you need more sensory neurons in some parts of your body than in others?

_____

_____

2. How do you use your sense of touch?

_____

3. Why is pain important ?

_____

4. What parts of your nervous system are involved when you touch something?

_____

SUGGESTIONS FOR FURTHER STUDY:

- Using the same equipment, determine the spacing of sensory neurons on the back, shoulder, and feet.

**Student Page –
Reflexes**

Name _____

Date _____

DESCRIPTION: In the space below, describe each of the reflexes you observed.

_____

_____

_____

_____

_____

_____

_____

_____

QUESTIONS:

1.

_____

_____

2. When people learn how to drive, they often say that they have developed good reflexes. Is this an accurate description of what they have learned? Explain your answer.

_____

_____

3. How do reflexes differ from habits?

_____

_____

4. What is the difference between a reflex and an reflex arc?

_____

_____

5. How are the reflexes you observed protective?

_____

_____

Student Page –
Conditioning

Name _____

Date _____

DESCRIPTION: In the space below make a slash every time your teacher says the word *write*.

_____

_____

_____

Count the number of slashes you made.

_____

QUESTIONS:

1. Did you continue to write after your teacher stopped saying the word *write*?

_____

2. In this activity, what was the original stimulus and what was the new stimulus?

_____

_____

3. Describe Pavlov's experiment with dogs.

_____

_____

_____

_____

4. What is meant by *conditioned behavior*?

_____

_____

5. How do people use conditioning to train animals?

_____

_____

Student Page – Habits

Name _____

Date _____

DESCRIPTION: Your teacher will dictate a paragraph. You are to copy this paragraph in the space provided, but you are not to cross the *t* or dot the *i* in any of the words.

_____

_____

_____

_____

_____

_____

_____

QUESTIONS:

1. Count up the number of crossed *t*'s and dotted *i*'s in your paragraph.

_____

_____

2. Why did you find it so difficult to write without crossing *t*'s and dotting *i*'s?

_____

_____

3. Describe how you were taught to write.

_____

_____

4. Describe four habits that you practice every day.

_____

_____

5. Why are habits important to us?

_____

_____

**Student Page –
Trial and Error**

Name

Date

DESCRIPTION: Record the amount of time it took you to solve the puzzle after each trial.

_____

_____

_____

QUESTIONS:

1. Why did it take less time after each trial?

    _____

    _____

2. Give an example of trial–and–error learning.

    _____

    _____

3. What are some other methods by which we learn?

    _____

    _____

4. Can animals learn by trial and error?

    _____

    _____

**Student Page –
The Learning Game**

Name _____

Date _____

DESCRIPTION:

1. In playing this game, how many items were the people in the game able to include in their list?

    _____

    _____

    _____

2. What factors were important in learning the items in the list?

    _____

    _____

QUESTIONS:

1. Was this a form of trial–and–error learning? Explain.

    _____

    _____

2. What factors might affect your score in this game?

    _____

    _____

3. If this game were played in a foreign language, how would it affect your score?

    _____

    _____

4. Did you enjoy this game? Did your attitude affect your score?

    _____

    _____

Learning Through Understanding

Name _____

Date _____

INTRODUCTION: Many factors affect our ability to learn things. In this activity we are going to compare our ability to memorize lists of words that have different amounts of meaning for us. We will see if it is easier to memorize words that have meaning than words that don't.

EQUIPMENT AND MATERIALS:

Paper   Pen or pencil

PROCEDURE:

1. Read through list 1 carefully three times. Without looking at the list, write down as many items on the list as you can remember in the order in which they appear.

2. Read list 2 three times, and follow the directions in procedure number 1.

3. Read list 3 carefully three times. Follow the directions in procedure 1.

4. Compare your lists with the original lists, and count the number of items you correctly remembered from each list.

1	2	3
bip	house	away
goz	cat	with
caj	this	recipes
lop	when	in
mot	dish	books
zub	shop	hunger
tox	cake	is
hib	flash	the
dib	sox	best
gok	mouse	of
fax	grab	cooks

CONCLUSIONS:

1. Which list did you remember the most words from?

    _____

2. Which list did you remember the least number of words from?

    _____

QUESTIONS:

1. How did memorizing list 3 differ from memorizing list 1?

    _____

2. How did memorizing list 3 differ from memorizing list 2?

    _____

    _____

3. What conclusions can you draw from this exercise?

    _____

    _____

4. Which of these lists would you consider the control? Why?

    _____

    _____

5. How can the information from this experiment help you in studying?

    _____

    _____

SUGGESTIONS FOR FURTHER STUDY:

- Devise an experiment to test the effect of conditions in a room such as light or noise on your ability to memorize words.

**Student Page –
Hormone Diseases**

Name _____

Date _____

DESCRIPTION:

For each photograph you saw, list in the chart below the disease demonstrated, a description of the symptoms, the gland involved, the name of the hormone involved, and whether the gland is oversecreted or undersecreted.

Dsease	Symptoms	Gland	Hormone	Oversecretion or Undersecretion

QUESTIONS:

1. What is a hormone?

   _____

   _____

2. What causes giantism?

   _____

   _____

3. What problems do giants have?

   _____

   _____

4. What is the cause of diabetes?

   _____

   _____

5. How is diabetes treated?

   _____

   _____

6. What are the functions of thyroxine?

   _____

   _____

7. Which diseases are associated with the thyroid gland?

   _____

   _____

8. Why do you need iodine in your diet?

   _____

   _____

Student Page –
Comparison of the Costs of
Generic and Brand-Name Drugs

Name _____

Date _____

DESCRIPTION:

Look at the list of drugs that your teacher has given you. Choose five drugs on the list, and determine the cost per dose for the brand-names and their generic counterparts. Determine the cost per dose by dividing the cost by number of units.

QUESTIONS:

1. Which is it more economical to buy — generic or brand name drugs?

    _____

    _____

2. On a prescription your doctor must indicate "dispense as written" or you may receive the generic drug. Which would you want to receive? Why?

    _____

    _____

3. Why do you think that brand-name drugs cost so much more than generic drugs?

    _____

    _____

4. What is the meaning of an "over-the-counter" drug?

    _____

    _____

5. Can you buy generic forms of "over-the-counter" drugs? Which are cheaper?

    _____

    _____

    _____

<u>Drug Labels</u>

Name _____

Date _____

INTRODUCTION: When we look at the label on a drug package, we see a great deal of print. Have you ever bothered to read all that information? It may be helpful. In this activity we are going to read and interpret labels from drug packages. You will read the labels from two over-the-counter drug packages and answer questions on the basis of the information you find.

EQUIPMENT AND MATERIALS:

Two drug labels

PROCEDURE:

1. Look at the first label, and record the following information in your data table:

    a. The name of the drug

    b. Indications

    c. Directions

    d. Warnings

    e. Drug interaction precautions

    f. Ingredients (active, other)

    g. Dosage (adults and children)

    h. Expiration date

2. Look at the second label and follow the directions listed in step 1.

Drug No. 1 Name	Drug No. 2 Name
INDICATIONS 1. 2. 3.	INDICATIONS 1. 2. 3.
DIRECTIONS 1. 2. 3.	DIRECTIONS 1. 2. 3.
WARNINGS 1. 2. 3.	WARNINGS 1. 2. 3.
DRUG INTERACTION PRECAUTIONS 1. 2. 3.	DRUG INTERACTION PRECAUTIONS 1. 2. 3.
INGREDIENTS Active Ingredients Other Ingredients	INGREDIENTS Active Ingredients Other Ingredients
DOSAGE	DOSAGE
EXPIRATION DATE	EXPIRATION DATE

QUESTIONS:

1. What information can you get from the indications listed on a drug label?

   _____

   _____

2. On the two labels you looked at, how did the indications differ?

   _____

   _____

3. Why does dosage differ for children and adults?

   _____

   _____

4. How would you expect the directions for a skin cream to differ from those for a cold pill?

   _____

   _____

5. Why is it important to read the warnings on the label of a drug package before using it?

   _____

   _____

6. Did any of the warnings on the labels you looked at apply to you or to one of your parents?

   _____

   _____

7. What are active ingredients?

   _____

   _____

8. Why must all ingredients — not just the active ingredients — be listed on a package?

   _____

   _____

9. Why are drug interaction precautions important?

    _____

    _____

10. How did the drug interaction precautions on the two labels differ?

    _____

    _____

11. Why is it important to note the temperature at which the drug should be stored?

    _____

    _____

12. What other information might you find on the package label?

    _____

    _____

SUGGESTIONS FOR FURTHER STUDY:

- Look at drug labels for prescription drugs to see if they contain the same information as over-the-counter drugs.
- Write a report on the functions of the Food and Drug Administration.

Student Page –
Model of the Diseased Lung

Name _____

Date _____

DESCRIPTION: Describe the appearance of the lung of a person with emphysema, and that of a person with lung cancer.

_____

_____

_____

_____

_____

_____

QUESTIONS:

1. What is the principal cause of emphysema?

_____

_____

2. What are the symptoms of emphysema?

_____

_____

3. What does the Surgeon General's warning on cigarette packs say?

_____

_____

4. In what ways may smoking be harmful to your health?

_____

_____

5. If a smoker stops smoking, will his lungs get better?

_____

_____

Student Page –
Destructive Distillation of a Cigarette

Name _____

Date _____

DESCRIPTION:

1. Describe the apparatus used in this demonstration.

   _____

   _____

   _____

2. Describe the appearance of the distillate.

   _____

   _____

   _____

QUESTIONS:

1. When a person smokes, what enters his lungs?

   _____

   _____

2. Is it better for a smoker to smoke low-tar cigarettes?

   _____

   _____

3. What are some ways people may stop smoking?

   _____

   _____

4. Why have so many laws restricting smoking been enacted recently?

   _____

   _____

5. In what ways is smoking harmful?

   _____

   _____

The Effect of Drugs on Heartbeat

Name _____

Date _____

INTRODUCTION: Drugs affect the body in many ways. Often the effects of drugs may be overlooked because of benefits in treating symptoms of disease. Drugs that people abuse, or drugs that are used only for the feeling they induce in us, also affect our bodies. In this activity we are going to determine the effects of a variety of drugs on the heartbeat of an invertebrate called *Daphnia*. We have chosen this organism because its heartbeat can be seen through a microscope.

Although one can't assume that the effects of a drug on an animal will be the same in humans, we can assume some similarities. In this activity, we assume that these drugs will have a similar effect on the human heart. We are not certain of this, however, and we do not know if the amounts of each drug that we are using will work in the same way in humans. This is why new drugs that are first tested on animals must eventually be tested on humans.

EQUIPMENT AND MATERIALS:

Depression slide
Daphnia culture
Medicine dropper
Drug solutions with
   medicine droppers

Pencil
Paper
Microscope
Lens paper

PROCEDURE:

1. Pick up your microscope and equipment as instructed by your teacher.

2. Prepare your microscope for use, as you have been taught to do.

3. Clean the depression slide with lens paper, before you use it.

4. Place a drop of water, containing one *Daphnia*, in the depression of your slide.

5. Place the slide on the stage of the microscope, and focus it under low power. Be very careful to use the coarseadjustment knob by turning it only toward you and not away from you. This slide is thicker than other slides you have used and is easier for you to hit with the objective.

6. As you watch the heart beating under the microscope, tap the pencil point on a piece of paper, so that you produce a dot for every heartbeat. Practice this for several seconds. Your partner will time you as you tap out the heartbeat of three 15–second intervals. Record your data in the data table. Find an average of the three 15–second time intervals. Multiply the average for 15 seconds by 4 to obtain the heartbeat rate for one minute.

7. Remove the slide form the stage of the microscope, and place it on a piece of paper towel. Wash two or three drops of the first drug solution over the *Daphnia* in the slide depression. Wipe up any overflow with the paper towel.

8. Place the slide back on the stage, refocus, and repeat step 6. Record your data in the data table.

9. Repeat steps 7–8 for each drug to be tested by you and your laboratory partner.

DATA TABLE

1. Control

HEARTBEAT RATE	
Fifteen–Second Intervals	Heartbeat Count
Interval 1	
Interval 2	
Interval 3	
T = Total of the three intervals	
A = Average of the intervals = T÷3	
Average beats for 1 minute = A x 4	

2. Drug 1 Name _____

HEARTBEAT RATE	
Fifteen–Second Intervals	**Heartbeat Count**
Interval 1	
Interval 2	
Interval 3	
T = Total of the three intervals	
A = Average of the intervals = T÷3	
Average beats for 1 minute = A x 4	

3. Drug 2 Name_____

HEARTBEAT RATE	
Fifteen–Second Intervals	**Heartbeat Count**
Interval 1	
Interval 2	
Interval 3	
T = Total of the three intervals	
A = Average of the intervals = T÷3	
Average beats for 1 minute = A x 4	

4.   Drug 3 Name _____

HEARTBEAT RATE	
Fifteen–Second Intervals	Heartbeat Count
Interval 1	
Interval 2	
Interval 3	
T = Total of the three intervals	
A = Average of the intervals = T÷3	
Average beats for 1 minute = A x 4	

CONCLUSIONS:

1.   What was the average heartbeat rate for *Daphnia* that you found?

   _____

2.   What was the class average heartbeat rate for *Daphnia*?

   _____

3.   Which drug had the greatest effect in speeding up heartbeat?

   _____

4.   Which drug had the greatest effect in slowing down heartbeat?

   _____

5.   Which drug had the least effect on heartbeat?

   _____

QUESTIONS:

1.   Did the drugs you expected to have the greatest effect on heartbeat affect heartbeat the most?

   _____

   _____

2. Why did we find an average heartbeat for 15 seconds instead of counting the heartbeat for only one 15–second interval?

_____

_____

3. What conclusions can you draw from this experiment?

_____

_____

4. If you were designing a package label for these drugs, what warnings would you list?

_____

_____

5. How did your results compare with the class averages?

_____

_____

6. What assumptions have we made in this experiment?

_____

_____

SUGGESTIONS FOR FURTHER STUDY:

- If time permits, test additional drugs to see their effect on heartbeat.

Student Page –
The Skin

Name _____

Date _____

DESCRIPTION: Describe the layers of the skin.

_____

_____

_____

_____

_____

QUESTIONS:

1. How does the skin protect us ?

    _____

    _____

2. Why must burn victims be extra cautious about infection?

    _____

    _____

3. If your skin protects you, how may germs enter your body?

    _____

    _____

4. In addition to protecting you from disease, what other functions does your skin have?

    _____

    _____

5. What do we mean when we say that a person is immune to a disease?

    _____

    _____

Student Page –
White Blood Cells

Name _____

Date _____

DESCRIPTION: Make a drawing of a white blood cell.

QUESTIONS:

1. How do white blood cells protect us from disease?

   _____

   _____

2. What are antibodies?

   _____

   _____

3. One kind of white blood cell, the phagocyte, is described as an "eating" cell. What does such a cell "eat"?

   _____

   _____

4. Why are people with AIDS susceptible to so many diseases?

   _____

   _____

5. What sorts of organisms do white blood cells attack?

   _____

   _____

Student Page –
Bacteria on Your Hands

Name _____

Date _____

DESCRIPTION: Describe the two agar plates.

_____

_____

_____

_____

_____

QUESTIONS:

1. Why did the agar plate have to be incubated?

_____

_____

2. Which hand contained fewer bacteria? Explain why this is so.

_____

_____

3. Why should you wash your hands before handling food or an open cut?

_____

_____

4. If there are so many bacteria on your hands, why don't you get sick more often?

_____

_____

5. In addition to your hands, where else could you find bacteria?

_____

_____

Student Page –   Name _____
Bacteria   Date _____

DESCRIPTION: Draw and label each type of bacteria that you observed.

QUESTIONS:

1. How are bacteria classified?

    _____

    _____

2. For each type of bacteria, list a disease caused by it.

    _____

    _____

3. What are spores? Why are they important?

    _____

    _____

4. How do bacteria cause decay?

    _____

    _____

**Student Page –
Testing Disinfectants**

Name _____

Date _____

DESCRIPTION:

1. Describe each of the agar plates after they were incubated.

    _____

    _____

    _____

    _____

    _____

2. Which disinfectant was most effective?

    _____

3. Which disinfectant was least effective?

    _____

QUESTIONS:

1. What is the purpose of a disinfectant?

    _____

2. Why was it necessary to incubate the plates?

    _____

3. What is agar?

    _____

4. What precautions did your teacher take in handling these plates?

    _____

    _____

Student Page –
The Presence of Bacteria

Name _____

Date _____

DESCRIPTION: Describe the appearance of each plate after incubation.

_____

_____

_____

_____

_____

QUESTIONS:

What can you conclude about the presence of bacteria in our environment?

_____

_____

2. What is a bacterial colony?

_____

_____

_____

3. What must be done to sterilize the surfaces in the room?

_____

_____

4. If you placed bacteria taken from one colony under the microscope, how many different kinds of bacteria would you see? Explain your answer.

_____

_____

5. What are spores?

_____

_____

Student Page –
The Effect of Penicillin on Bacteria

Name _____

Date _____

DESCRIPTION: Describe the two plates.

_____

_____

_____

_____

QUESTIONS:

1. How can you account for the difference between the two plates?

    _____

    _____

2. How do we know that the difference is due to the effect of penicillin on bacteria?

    _____

    _____

3. What is an antibiotic?

    _____

    _____

4. What are examples of other antibiotics besides penicillin?

    _____

    _____

5. How was penicillin discovered?

    _____

    _____

6. Why don't we use antibiotics to treat viruses?

    _____

    _____

Student Page – Parasitic Worms

Name _____

Date _____

DESCRIPTION:

1. Describe the worms that you observed.

    _____

    _____

    _____

2. Describe the encysted trichina worm

    _____

    _____

QUESTIONS:

1. For each worm you described, tell how it affects humans.

    _____

    _____

    _____

2. What is a parasite?

    _____

    _____

3. How may a tapeworm enter your body?

    _____

    _____

4. How does a hookworm enter the human body?

    _____

    _____

5. Why is it important to cook pork well?

    _____

    _____

Bacteria

Name _____

Date _____

INTRODUCTION: Bacteria are everywhere: in the air, on your hair, on objects, on your skin. In this activity we are going to investigate the places bacteria grow, by trying to grow bacteria taken from these places. Think about the places you think it is most likely for bacteria to grow in. We will take samples from these places and attempt to grow them on agar plates. For bacteria to grow they must have a source of food and the proper temperature. We will grow the bacteria in petri dishes that contain a nutrient medium, and we'll place them in an incubator to keep them at the correct temperature. In a few days we will look at the plates to see if bacteria have grown.

EQUIPMENT AND MATERIALS:

Six petri dishes with nutrient agar   Three cotton swabs
Masking tape   Isotonic salt solution
Marking pencil

PROCEDURE:

1. Take one sterile petri dish, and seal it with masking tape around the edge. Using the marking pencil, write the word *control.*

2. Open a sterile petri dish, and place a hair on it. Seal it with masking tape. Using the marking pencil, label it *hair.*

3. Open a sterile petri dish, and press your fingertips into the agar. Close and seal the petri dish. Using the marking pencil, label it *fingers.*

4. Dip a cotton swab in the isotonic solution. Rub it on the surface of the object you suspect contains bacteria. Brush the cotton swab across the agar in the petri dish. Seal and label the dish as you have in procedures 1–3.

5. Prepare two more petri dishes in the same manner as in procedure 4. Use two different sources of bacteria.

6. Place your initials on the plates to identify yours. Follow your teacher's directions for collecting the petri dishes. They will be placed upside down in the incubator.

7. Following your teacher's directions, collect your incubated plates. Observe each of the petri dishes, and describe the bacteria growing in each one. Describe the shape, color, and texture of the bacterial cultures you observe.

OBSERVATIONS:

1. control

_____

_____

_____

2. hair

_____

_____

3. fingers

_____

_____

_____

4. _____

_____

_____

5. _____

_____

_____

6. _____

_____

_____

_____

QUESTIONS:

1. Why is it important to seal the petri dishes?

   _____

   _____

2. What is contained in the nutrient agar?

   _____

   _____

3. What is a sterile petri dish?

   _____

   _____

4. How is a petri dish sterilized?

   _____

   _____

5. In what ways did the bacterial colonies look alike?

   _____

   _____

6. How did the bacterial colonies look different?

   _____

   _____

7. Did you find bacteria in all of the places you expected to find them?

   _____

   _____

SUGGESTIONS FOR FURTHER STUDY:

- Look at plates of bacteria to which antibiotics have been added. How do antibiotics affect bacteria?
- Write a report on the effects of fungi on bacteria.

Student Page –
Sperm and Egg Cells

Name _____

Date _____

DESCRIPTION:

In the space below, draw the sperm cell and the egg cell.

          Sperm cell   Egg cell

QUESTIONS:

1. Which is larger — the sperm cell or the egg cell? How can you account for this?

   _____

   _____

2. How is the sperm cell adapted for locomotion?

   _____

   _____

3. What occurs during fertilization?

   _____

   _____

4. What is the male gamete? Where is it produced?

   _____

   _____

5. What is the female gamete? Where is it produced?

   _____

   _____

6. How many sperm cells can fertilize an egg?

   _____

**Student Page –
The Male Reproductive System**

Name _____

Date _____

DESCRIPTION:

Label the parts of the male reproductive system.

QUESTIONS:

1. Why are the testes located in the scrotum?

_____

_____

_____

_____

_____

_____

_____

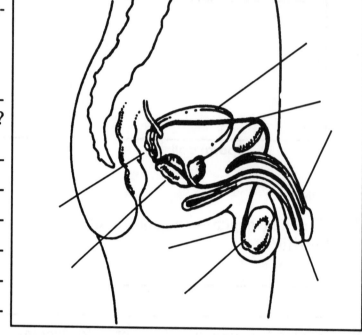

Diagram 10-1 *Male reproductive system*

2. Where are sperm cells produced?

_____

_____

3. What is the function of the seminal fluid?

_____

_____

4. Where is seminal fluid produced?

_____

_____

5. How does semen leave the penis?

_____

_____

6.   What is a vasectomy?

_____

_____

7.   What is a circumcision?

_____

_____

Student Page –
The Female Reproductive System

Name _____

Date _____

DESCRIPTION: Label the parts of the female reproductive system.

QUESTIONS:

1. Where is the egg produced?

   _____

   _____

   _____

   _____

   _____

   _____

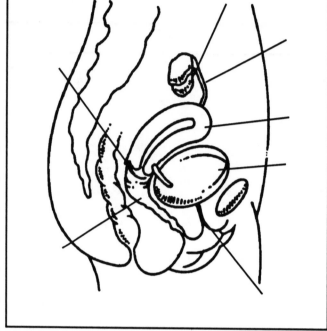

Diagram 10-2 *Female reproductive system*

2. Where does fertilization occur?

   _____

   _____

3. How does the size of the uterus compare with the size of the uterus in a pregnant woman?

   _____

   _____

4. Which parts of the reproductive system undergo the greatest change during pregnancy?

   _____

   _____

5. Trace the path of the sperm to the egg.

    _____

    _____

6. What is the function of the uterus?

    _____

    _____

Student Page –
The Menstrual Cycle

Name _____

Date _____

DESCRIPTION:

Briefly describe what occurs during each of the four phases of the menstrual cycle.

_____

_____

_____

_____

QUESTIONS:

1.　What is the average length of the menstrual cycle?

_____

_____

2.　What factors may disrupt the menstrual cycle?

_____

_____

3.　Why must the uterine lining be built up each month?

_____

_____

4.　Which glands produce the hormones that regulate the menstrual cycle?

_____

_____

5.　What is the function of estrogen?

_____

_____

6.　How does progesterone affect the menstrual cycle?

_____

_____

Student Page –
Methods of Birth Control

Name _____

Date _____

Study the chart of methods of birth control, and answer the following questions:

1. Which methods of birth control are most effective?

   _____

   _____

2. Which methods of birth control are least effective?

   _____

   _____

3. Which methods work by preventing sperm from meeting egg?

   _____

   _____

4. Which method may involve side effects?

   _____

   _____

5. Which method of birth control works by fooling the body into thinking it is pregnant?

   _____

   _____

**Student Page –
Cleavage**

Name

Date

DESCRIPTION: Draw a two–cell stage, a four–cell stage, a blastula, and a gastrula.

QUESTIONS:

1. As cleavage occurs, what happens to the size of the cells?

   _____

   _____

2. What would happen if, during the two–cell stage, the two cells separated?

   _____

   _____

3. How many layers of cells are there in the blastula?

   _____

   _____

4. Name the three germ layers that are found in the gastrula.

   _____

   _____

5. For each germ layer, list three organs that will form.

   _____

   _____

Student Page –
The Female Reproductive System

Name _____

Date _____

DESCRIPTION: Describe the changes that occur to the female reproductive system during pregnancy?

_____

_____

_____

_____

QUESTIONS:

1. Pregnant females urinate more frequently than normal. How can you account for this?

    _____

    _____

2. How does the fetus usually position itself before birth?

    _____

    _____

    _____

    _____

3. How does the fetus receive food?

    _____

    _____

4. What is the function of the amnion?

    _____

    _____

5. What is the function of the placenta?

    _____

    _____

    _____

    _____

6. What does it mean when we say a woman's water has broken?

    _____

    _____

7. What starts labor?

    _____

    _____

8. What may happen if the fetus is in the wrong position before birth?

    _____

    _____

Cleavage

Name _____

Date _____

INTRODUCTION: After fertilization, the fertilized egg, which is called the *zygote* undergoes a series of rapid cell divisions known as cleavage. Cleavage in the human is difficult to follow because of the special modifications necessary for the formation of the placenta. We are going to observe cleavage in starfish eggs, because it is easy to see the stages of cleavage in this organism.

EQUIPMENT AND MATERIALS:

Microscope
Light source
Lens paper
Prepared slide of cleavage in starfish eggs

PROCEDURE:

1. When instructed by your teacher, pick up your microscope and other equipment.

2. Prepare your microscope for use, as you have been instructed to do.

3. Using the lens paper, clean the prepared slide before you use it.

4. Place the slide on the stage, and focus it under low power. (Remember to watch the stage while you lower the objective with the coarse–adjustment knob and to focus only by turning the coarse–adjustment knob toward you.)

5. Look for a single egg, a two–cell stage, and a four–cell stage. Draw each of these in the appropriate space, and label each drawing.

6. Look for a blastula, and draw it in the appropriate space. Be sure to label the drawing.

7. Look for a gastrula, and draw it in the appropriate space. Be sure to label the diagram.

OBSERVATIONS:

Drawing of the zygote, and two–cell and four–cell stages in cleavage

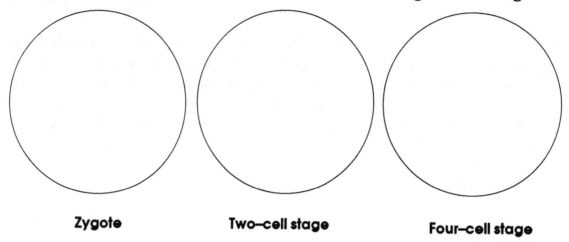

Zygote   **Two–cell stage**   **Four–cell stage**

Drawings of the blastula and gastrula

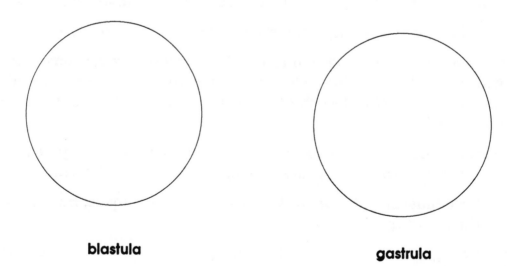

blastula   **gastrula**

QUESTIONS:

1. Do the cells in each successive stage remain the same size or do they change?

    _____

    _____

2. How would you describe the blastula?

    _____

    _____

3. What takes place during the formation of the gastrula?

    _____

    _____

4. How many layers of cells do you see in a gastrula? Name them.

    _____

    _____

5. List each of the germ layers and three organs that each will form.

    _____

    _____

    _____

SUGGESTIONS FOR FURTHER STUDY:

- Count the number of eggs in each stage of cleavage, on your slide

Dissection of a Pig's Uterus

Name _____

Date _____

INTRODUCTION: Mammals have evolved special adaptations for the development of the embryo in the uterus of its mother. In this activity we will study the fetal pig in its mother's uterus.

EQUIPMENT AND MATERIALS:

Preserved pig's uterus   Scalpel
Dissecting pan   Probe
Scissors

PROCEDURE:

Your teacher will dissect the pig's uterus. You are to observe the position of the embryo in the uterus, and the umbilical cord, the placenta, the amnion and the chorion.

OBSERVATIONS

Label the structures in the diagram below

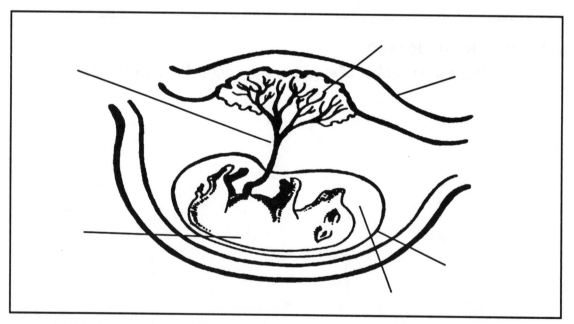

Diagram 10-3 *A pig fetus in place within the uterus*

QUESTIONS:

1. What is the function of the amnion?

   _____

   _____

2. Why is it safer to sample the chorionic villi instead of amnionic fluid to determine the genetic makeup of the fetus?

   _____

   _____

3. Describe the function of the placenta?

   _____

   _____

4. Is it possible for maternal blood and fetal blood to mix? Why or why not?

   _____

   _____

5. How does the pig's uterus differ from the human's uterus?

   _____

   _____

6. List three substances that can pass from the mother's blood to the fetus.

   _____

   _____

7. A baby is born immune to the diseases its mother is immune to. How can you account for this?

   _____

   _____

SUGGESTIONS FOR FURTHER STUDY:

- Look at a slide of amnionic fluid. Do you see any cells in it?
- Prepare a report on caesarian sections.

**Student Page –
Family Resemblance**

Name _____

Date _____

DESCRIPTION: Which photographs show the greatest family resemblance?

_____

_____

_____

_____

QUESTIONS:

1. How can you account for the family resemblances you observed?

_____

_____

2. Do all the children of the same parents look alike? How can you account for these differences?

_____

_____

3. Which of your relatives do you look most like?

_____

_____

4. What is it that we inherit form our parents that controls what we look like?

_____

_____

5. Do both of your parents contribute equally to your heredity? Explain your answer.

_____

_____

Student Page –
A Comparison of Mitosis and Meiosis

Name _____

Date _____

DESCRIPTION:

In the table below, compare the changes that occur during mitosis and the changes that occur during meiosis.

MITOSIS	MEIOSIS

QUESTIONS:

1. Which process produces gametes?

    _____

2. At the end of meiosis, how many cells are produced?

    _____

3. At the end of mitosis, how many cells are produced?

    _____

4. During which process are chromosome pairs separated?

    _____

5. At the end of mitosis, are chromosomes single–stranded or double–stranded?

    _____

Student Page –
Mitosis

Name _____

Date _____

DESCRIPTION:

1. Draw a diagram showing what occurs during each phase of mitosis.

2. For each drawing, list what takes place.

QUESTIONS:

1. What is meant by the replication of a chromosome? When does it occur?

_____

_____

2. What is the role of the spindle fibers in mitosis?

_____

_____

3. What is the purpose of mitosis?

_____

_____

4. Which processes in the body depend on mitosis?

_____

_____

Student Page –
The Trait Game

Name _____

Date _____

DESCRIPTION: List the traits that your teacher used to identify people in the room:

_____

_____

_____

_____

QUESTIONS:

1. What is a trait?

_____

_____

2. What are examples of traits that we can easily see?

_____

_____

3. What are traits that we can not easily see?

_____

_____

4. Why is the study of traits important?

_____

_____

5. How do we inherit our traits?

_____

_____

Student Page –
The Model of DNA

Name

Date

DESCRIPTION:

1. Describe the structure of DNA

_____

_____

2. Describe how DNA molecules replicate.

_____

_____

3. List the four–base pair combinations in DNA.

_____

_____

QUESTIONS:

1. How does DNA store information?

_____

_____

2. Where is DNA found in the cell?

_____

_____

3. Describe the parts of a nucleotide that make up DNA.

_____

_____

4. Why are people different from one another?

_____

_____

**Student Page –
Codons**

Name _____

Date _____

DESCRIPTION: Describe how DNA regulates the assembly of amino acids into proteins.

_____

_____

_____

_____

_____

_____

_____

_____

_____

_____

_____

_____

QUESTIONS:

1. What is a codon?

   _____

2. How many bases make up a codon?

   _____

3. How many different codons are there?

   _____

4. How would changing one codon affect the proteins that a cell makes?

   _____

   _____

Student Page –
The Hybrid Coin Toss

Name _____

Date _____

DESCRIPTION:

In the table below, record the number of head/head, head/tail and tail/tail tosses.

HEAD/HEAD (pure dominant)	HEAD/TAIL (hybrid)	TAIL/TAIL (pure recessive)

QUESTIONS:

1. How did the results compare with the predicted results of such a cross?

   _____

   _____

2. Did the ratios change as you continued to toss coins? Why?

   _____

   _____

3. How would you explain that two people with dark hair have three blond children?

   _____

   _____

Student Page –   Name _____
Colorblindness Test   Date _____

DESCRIPTION:

1. Describe the chart that is used to test for colorblindness.

    _____

    _____

    _____

2. Why can't a colorblind person see the number on the chart?

    _____

    _____

QUESTIONS:

1. How is colorblindness inherited?

    _____

2. Can a boy inherit colorblindness from his father? Explain your answer.

    _____

    _____

3. What do we mean when we say that colorblindness is sex linked?

    _____

4. What is another trait that is sex linked?

    _____

5. Why is it unusual for a girl to be colorblind?

    _____

6. Can a colorblind person see colors? Explain your answer.

    _____

    _____

Student Page –
Linkage

Name _____

Date _____

DESCRIPTION:

Draw a diagram to show how linked genes would appear on a chromosome.

QUESTIONS:

1. How could you explain the fact that redheaded people often have freckles?

   _____

2. Why is the inheritance of sex–linked traits different from other examples of linkage?

   _____

3. Can genes on different chromosomes be linked? Explain your answer.

   _____

4. If two genes are linked, will they be inherited independently?

   _____

**Student Page –
Fruit Flies**

Name _____

Date _____

DESCRIPTION:

1. Describe how the fruit flies are kept.

    _____

    _____

2. List the traits that you can observe by looking at the fruit fly.

    _____

    _____

    _____

QUESTIONS:

1. Why are fruit flies used in genetics studies?

    _____

    _____

2. What is the advantage of using a fruit fly as a laboratory animal instead of an elephant?

    _____

    _____

3. What advantage is there in using a fruit fly instead of a human to study inheritance?

    _____

    _____

**Student Page –
P. T. C. Paper**

Name _____

Date _____

DESCRIPTION:

1. Describe how P. T. C. paper tastes to you?

    _____

    _____

2. Are you a taster or a nontaster?

    _____

3. Were most people in your class tasters or nontasters?

    _____

QUESTIONS:

1. Tasting is a dominant trait. What does that tell you about the possible genotypes of your parents? Explain your answer.

    _____

    _____

2. John is a nontaster, and his mother and father are tasters.

    a. What is the genotype of each of his parents?

    _____

    _____

    b. What are the chances of his brothers and sisters being tasters?

    _____

    _____

3. How does the inheritance of tongue–rolling compare with the inheritance of tasting?

    _____

    _____

Student Page –
Human Karyotypes

Name _____

Date _____

DESCRIPTION:

1. Cut out the chromosomes from the plate your teacher gave you.

2. Place the chromosomes on the chart so that the centromere of each chromosome is on the line. When you pair up the chromosomes pay attention to the location of the centromere and the length of the arms.

3. Arrange the pairs of chromosomes on the chart, from the longest to shortest. Place the five longest pairs on the top line, and continue arranging them until all of the pairs have been placed on the chart. Place the sex chromosomes in the lower right corner.

4. Count the number of pairs to make certain you have placed 23 pairs.

_____

_____

_____

_____   _____

sex chromosomes

Law of Chance

Name _____

Date _____

INTRODUCTION: You have learned to use the Punnett square to predict the results of a cross between two individuals who are hybrid for a trait. In this activity we will simulate a situation in which a pair of individuals mates many times. We will observe whether this results in the same ratios as we have predicted.

EQUIPMENT AND MATERIALS:

Two dishes, each containing 30 black beans and 30 brown beans.

Procedure: This activity requires three active participants: two to select beans and one to record the results.

1. Each person with a dish of beans is to pick one bean without looking. Each will then call out the color of the bean he or she has picked.

2. The recorder will record the results of each cross in the data table. Let's arbitrarily decide to call the black bean the dominant trait (B) and the brown bean the recessive trait (b)

3. At the end of each 20 crosses, count and record the results.

OBSERVATIONS:

BB	Bb	bb
total	total	total
total	total	total
total	total	total
TOTALS		

QUESTIONS:

1. How did the results compare with the predicted results of such a cross?

    _____

2. Did the ratios change much during the different intervals for which you counted the results? Why?

    _____

    _____

3. How would you explain that two people with dark hair have three blond children?

    _____

    _____

SUGGESTIONS FOR FURTHER STUDY:

   * Try this experiment, but change the gene pool of one of the people by using different beans, e. g. , all one color. How does this change the results?

Preparing a Family Tree

Name _____

Date _____

INTRODUCTION: A family tree is a visual representation of the inheritance of a trait in a family. In this activity you will prepare your own family tree for one trait, and then try to draw conclusions from it. Study the simple family tree below as a guide to setting up such a chart for your family.

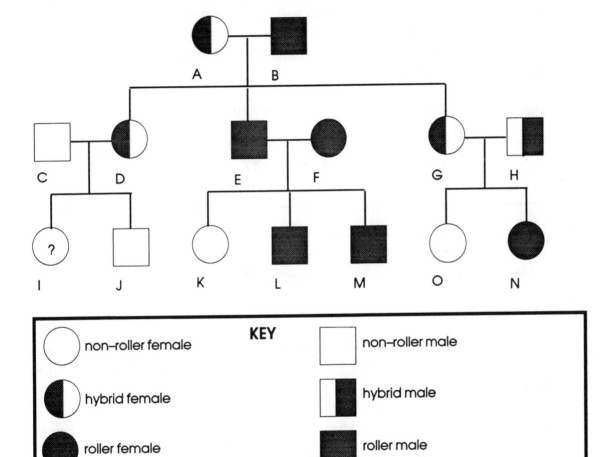

KEY

○ non–roller female

◐ hybrid female

● roller female

□ non–roller male

◧ hybrid male

■ roller male

EQUIPMENT AND MATERIALS:

Data sheet

Paper

PROCEDURE:

1. Prepare a key to indicate the symbols you are using in this family tree. Be sure to indicate females with and without the trait and males with and without the trait.

2. Look at the data you have collected or the data provided by your teacher, to determine how many generations you will study and the number and sex of each individual in each generation. On the basis of this information, prepare the family tree.

3. Using the data, fill in the appropriate information for each individual on your family tree. Use the symbols in your key to indicate the phenotype of each individual.

4. You may write the name of each individual below the symbol representing that persons, or you can indicate each one with a number or letter. If you use a number or letter for each individual you may wish to prepare a list of the people represented and the number or letter that indicates each person.

CONCLUSIONS:

1. According to your family tree, which individuals exhibit the dominant trait and which the recessive trait?

   _____

   _____

2. Which trait do you think is the recessive trait? What evidence do you have for this?

   _____

   _____

3. Which individuals in your family do you think are hybrids for this trait?

   _____

   _____

4. What evidence can you give to support your answer to question 3?

   _____

   _____

QUESTIONS:

Base your answers to these questions on the family tree presented in the introduction.

1. Why don't we know whether person *I* is pure dominant or hybrid?

   _____

   _____

2. What is the probability of couple *G & H* having a third child who is a nonroller?

   _____

   _____

3. How do we know that person *D* is a hybrid?

   _____

   _____

4. What are the genotypes of persons *H*, *N*, and *O*?

   _____

   _____

5. What are the phenotypes of persons *H*, *N*, and *O*?

   _____

   _____

6. If person *K* marries a nonroller, what is the likelihood of their having a child who is a nonroller? Explain your answer.

   _____

   _____

7. How many grandsons do *A* and *B* have?

   _____

   _____

SUGGESTIONS FOR FURTHER STUDY:

- Collect additional data on another trait, and construct another family tree.

**Student Page –
Down's Syndrome**

Name _____

Date _____

DESCRIPTION: How does the karyotype of a person with Down's syndrome differ from that of a normal person?

_____

_____

_____

_____

_____

QUESTIONS:

1. What is nondisjunction?

_____

2. When does nondisjunction occur?

_____

3. What are some other syndromes caused by nondisjunction?

_____

4. How can a doctor test to find out if a fetus has Down's syndrome?

_____

5. Which group of women is at greatest risk of having a child with Down's syndrome?

_____

_____

Student Page –
The Geiger Counter

Name _____

Date _____

DESCRIPTION: Describe how a Geiger counter works.

_____

_____

_____

_____

QUESTIONS:

1. Why must you protect yourself from exposure to radiation?

    _____

    _____

2. If you have an x–ray at the doctor's office or the dentist's office, how
    does the doctor protect you from the radiation?

    _____

    _____

3. What are some other examples of mutagenic agents?

    _____

    _____

4. What is a mutation?

    _____

    _____

5. What is a carcinogen?

    _____

    _____

6. To what sources of radiation might you be exposed?

    _____

    _____

**Student Page –
Chromosomal Mutations**

Name

Date

DESCRIPTION: In the space below, draw diagrams to show what occurs during an inversion, a deletion, a translocation, nondisjunction, and crossing over.

QUESTIONS:

1. How does a chromosomal mutation differ from a gene mutation?

   _____

   _____

2. Which would you expect to have a greater effect on an individual — a chromosomal mutation or a gene mutation? Explain your answer.

   _____

   _____

Student Page –
Fossil Formation

Name _____

Date _____

DESCRIPTION: Describe the method or methods your teacher used to demonstrate the formation of fossils.

_____

_____

_____

_____

_____

QUESTIONS:

1. How do fossils form in sedimentary rock?

_____

_____

2. How might the imprint of an animal or a plant become preserved?

_____

_____

3. What sort of animals might be preserved in amber?

_____

_____

4. What can we learn form fossils?

_____

_____

5. Why are fossils considered evidence of evolution?

_____

_____

6. In addition to the methods you have observed, how else might fossils form?

_____

_____

Student Page –
Fossils

Name _____

Date _____

DESCRIPTION: Describe the fossils you saw in class.

_____

_____

_____

_____

_____

_____

_____

_____

QUESTIONS:

1. List three methods of fossil formation.

_____

_____

2. How can scientists determine the age of a fossil?

_____

_____

3. What do fossils tell us about the animals and plants on this planet?

_____

_____

4. Why are fossils usually found only in sedimentary rock?

_____

_____

5. What do we mean when we say life has evolved?

_____

_____

**Student Page –
Comparative Embryology**

Name _____

Date _____

DESCRIPTION: After looking at the embryos that your teacher has shown you, describe how they are similar and how they are different.

_____

_____

_____

_____

_____

QUESTIONS:

1. Were you able to tell one embryo from another? Why was it difficult to do so?

_____

_____

2. What conclusion can you draw from the fact that all vertebrate embryos look alike?

_____

_____

3. What do we mean when we say that vertebrates share a common ancestor?

_____

_____

4. What are the characteristics of a vertebrate?

_____

_____

5. Which groups of animals are classified as vertebrates?

_____

_____

Student Page –
Vestigial Structures

Name _____

Date _____

DESCRIPTION: List and describe the vestigial structures found in humans.

_____

_____

_____

_____

_____

_____

_____

QUESTIONS:

1. Define what is meant by a vestigial structure.

    _____

    _____

2. What conclusion can we draw from our study of vestigial structures?

    _____

    _____

3. In what way do vestigial structures support the idea of common ancestry?

    _____

    _____

4. By studying vestigial structures in humans, what can we conclude about our ancestors?

    _____

    _____

Comparative Anatomy

Name _____

Date _____

INTRODUCTION: In this activity we will study and compare the skeletons of different vertebrates. We hope to see in what ways they are similar and in what ways they are different.

EQUIPMENT AND MATERIALS:

Samples of vertebrate skeletons

PROCEDURE:

1. Around the room is a series of laboratory stations. At each station is a vertebrate skeleton. Your teacher will instruct you which station to begin at, and the order in which you are to visit each station.

2. When you get to a station, you are to record the name of the animal, and the class of vertebrates it belongs to (fish, amphibian, reptile, bird, or mammal).

3. You are to write a brief description of each animal's skeleton, trying to note both similarities to other vertebrates and differences from them. If you wish, you may draw a small sketch of the specimen to help you remember its appearance.

OBSERVATIONS

Station number	Animal's name	Vertebrate class

DESCRIPTION

Station number	Animal's name	Vertebrate class

DESCRIPTION

Station number	Animal's name	Vertebrate class

DESCRIPTION

Station number	Animal's name	Vertebrate class

DESCRIPTION

Station number	Animal's name	Vertebrate class

DESCRIPTION

Station number	Animal's name	Vertebrate class

DESCRIPTION

Station number	Animal's name	Vertebrate class

DESCRIPTION

Station number	Animal's name	Vertebrate class

DESCRIPTION

CONCLUSIONS:

1. In what ways are the rib cage and pelvis (hip bones) similar among the vertebrates you studied?

   _____

   _____

2. How are the forelimbs of the animals you studied similar? How are they different?

   _____

   _____

3. Which animals seemed most alike to you? Why?

   _____

   _____

4. Which animals seemed most unlike the other vertebrates? Can you suggest a reason for this?

   _____

   _____

5. Which animal had a skeleton that was most like human's?

   _____

   _____

6. On the basis of your observations, which vertebrate do you think was the first to evolve?

   _____

   _____

QUESTIONS:

1. Of the animals whose skeletons you studied, which were mammals? In what ways are these animals similar?

    _____

    _____

    _____

2. Do we, as humans, have all of the characteristics of other mammals? Explain.

    _____

    _____

    _____

3. What can we learn from the study of comparative anatomy?

    _____

    _____

    _____

4. Choose an animal that lives in water and explain how it is specialized to live in water.

    _____

    _____

    _____

5. How does a land animal differ from an animal that lives in water?

    _____

    _____

    _____

SUGGESTIONS FOR FURTHER STUDY:

- For each of the animals whose skeletons you looked at, tell how its skeleton is adapted for its type of life.

Student Page –
Mimicry and Camouflage

Name _____

Date _____

DESCRIPTION:

1. Describe the examples of mimicry and camouflage you saw.

    _____

    _____

    _____

2. How do these characteristics help the animal survive?

    _____

    _____

3. Suggest an explanation of how these adaptations developed.

    _____

    _____

    _____

    _____

QUESTIONS:

1. Define mimicry.

    _____

    _____

2. How might coloration help an insect to survive?

    _____

    _____

3. Would these insects survive in a different environment such as a city?
    Explain your answer.

    _____

    _____

    _____

Student Page –   Name _____
Overproduction   Date _____

DESCRIPTION:

1. How many eggs did one female produce?

    _____

2. How many seeds did one plant produce?

    _____

QUESTIONS:

1. Why does one female produce so many eggs?

    _____

    _____

2. What is the advantage of overproduction?

    _____

    _____

3. Do all of these eggs survive? Explain your answer.

    _____

    _____

4. Because more individuals than can survive are produced, what determines which survive?

    _____

    _____

5. What is meant by the struggle for survival?

    _____

    _____

6. What is meant by survival of the fittest?

    _____

    _____

    _____

**Student Page –
Darwin's Finches**

Name _____

Date _____

DESCRIPTION: Describe the shape of the beak of each variety of finch, and tell what that finch eats.

_____

_____

_____

_____

_____

_____

_____

QUESTIONS:

1. How can you explain the variety of beak types found in the finch population?

    _____

    _____

2. What does the shape of the beak have to do with the bird's diet?

    _____

    _____

3. How are these birds adapted to different diets?

    _____

    _____

4. How did Charles Darwin explain the variety of finches found on the Galapagos Islands?

    _____

    _____

Student Page –
Adaptation

Name _____

Date _____

DESCRIPTION: For each mammal skull you were shown, describe the shape of its teeth, and tell what the animal eats.

_____

_____

_____

_____

_____

_____

_____

_____

_____

_____

QUESTIONS:

1. What can we determine about an animal's diet by studying its teeth?

_____

_____

2. How are an animal's teeth and jaws an adaptation for its diet?

_____

_____

3. Which animals have similar diets?

_____

_____

4. Compare the teeth of animals with similar diets.

_____

_____

Student Page –
Plaster Cast of Bird's Feet

Name _____

Date _____

DESCRIPTION:

1. Describe how the plaster casts were taken.

    _____

    _____

    _____

    _____

2. Describe the shape of the feet.

    _____

    _____

    _____

    _____

QUESTIONS:

1. For each foot shape, tell what you think it is adapted for.

    _____

    _____

2. How does the shape of a bird's foot help it to survive?

    _____

    _____

3. Why is variation necessary for evolution to occur?

    _____

    _____

4. What is the survival value of each type of foot?

    _____

    _____

Variations in a Small Population

Name _____

Date _____

INTRODUCTION: Members of the same species resemble one another in many ways. They also differ from one another in many ways. The differences we observe among individuals of the same species are called *variations*. In this activity we will observe variations in the hand spans of members of this class.

EQUIPMENT AND MATERIALS:

Metric ruler
Pencil

PROCEDURE:

1. Using a metric ruler, measure the hand span of your left hand, from the tip of your thumb to the tip of your pinkie. See Diagram 12–1. Write your hand span and gender on a piece of paper and pass it up to your teacher, as you have been instructed to do.

2. After all of the data has been collected for the class, transfer this data to your data table.

3. Prepare two graphs of the class results. One graph plots the number of students with each sized hand span against the hand span for boys and one for girls.

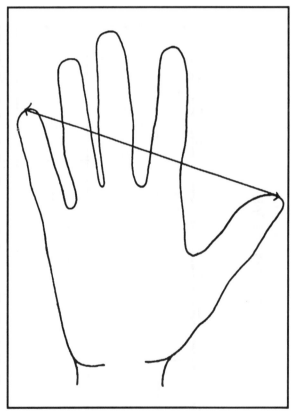

Diagram 12-1 *Measuring hand span*

OBSERVATIONS

DATA TABLE

Total number of hands spans with the same measurement	15 cm	16 cm	17 cm	18 cm	19 cm	20 cm	21 cm	22 cm	23 cm	24 cm	25 cm	26 cm	27 cm	28 cm
Males														
Females														

GRAPH 1 – Boys

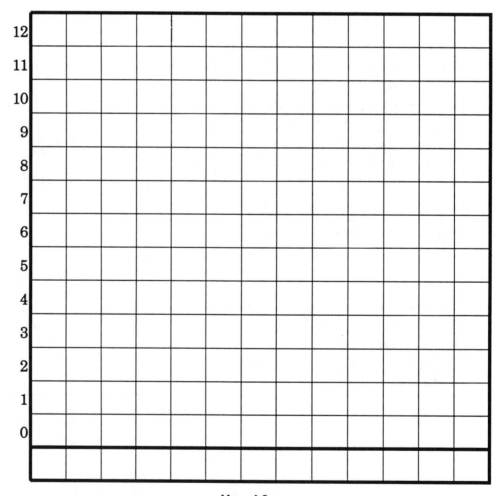

Hand Span

GRAPH 2 – Girls

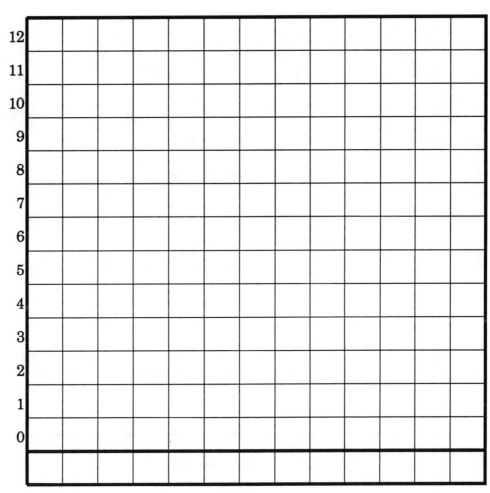

Hand Span

CONCLUSIONS:

1. Are the hand spans of all the students in your class the same?

    _____

2. Why did we record the hand spans of boys and girls separately?

    _____

3. Which hand span occurs most often among boys?

    _____

4. Which hand span occurs most often among girls?

    _____

5. What is the total range of hand spans in your class?

    _____

6. Are all the students in your class the same age?

_____

7. If we recorded data only for students who are the same age, would
    our data have been more reliable? Why?

_____

QUESTIONS

1. How would you define the term *variation*?

_____

2. List five other variations that you can observe among people in the
    class.

_____

3. What are two variations in humans that make us different from other
    animals?

_____

4. Why are variations so important to Darwin's theory of natural selec-
    tion?

_____

5. How can we account for variation?

_____

6. Why do organisms that reproduce sexually have more variations than
    those which reproduce asexually?

_____

SUGGESTIONS FOR FURTHER STUDY:

- Develop a procedure to collect data about other variations that
  occur in your class population.

Student Page –   Name _____
The Effects of Light and
Minerals on Plant Growth   Date _____

DESCRIPTION:

1. Describe the effects of different lighting conditions on the plant.

    _____

    _____

    _____

    _____

2. Describe the effects of different amounts of water on the plant.

    _____

    _____

3. Describe the effects of different minerals on the growth of the plant.

    _____

    _____

QUESTIONS:

1. What are the abiotic factors in a plant's environment?

    _____

    _____

2. Which minerals seem to have the greatest effect on plant growth?

    _____

    _____

3. How does the amount of water in the environment affect a plant?

    _____

    _____

4. How does a plant affect the physical environment?

    _____

    _____

**Student Page –
Reaction of Different
Plants to a Similar Environment**

Name _____

Date _____

DESCRIPTION:

1. Describe the conditions under which the plants were grown.

    _____

    _____

    _____

2. Name and describe the plants that were grown under these conditions.

    _____

    _____

3. Which plant is best adapted to this environment? What is its natural habitat?

    _____

    _____

QUESTIONS:

1. Why will a desert plant have difficulty growing in a tropical rain forest?

    _____

    _____

2. Why will a plant that grows in a rain forest have difficulty growing in a desert?

    _____

    _____

3. How does the physical environment determine the plants that grow in a particular environment?

    _____

    _____

    _____

Student Page –
Terrarium–Herbarium

Name _____

Date _____

DESCRIPTION: Describe the conditions and types of organism growing in each of the terraria your teacher has shown you.

_____

_____

_____

_____

_____

_____

_____

_____

QUESTIONS:

1. How are the organisms in each terrarium adapted to their environment?

   _____

   _____

2. How do organisms affect their physical environment?

   _____

   _____

3. How do plants affect the animals that may grow in a particular environment?

   _____

   _____

4. How do animals affect the plants that may grow in a particular environment?

   _____

   _____

**Student Page –
A Balanced Aquarium**

Name _____

Date _____

DESCRIPTION: List the organisms that are found in the aquarium and describe their role in the food chain.

_____

_____

_____

_____

_____

QUESTIONS:

1. How are materials recycled in this aquarium?

_____

_____

2. What is the source of energy in this aquarium?

_____

_____

3. What would happen if you placed the aquarium in a dark closet?

_____

_____

4. Which organisms are the producers?

_____

_____

Habitats

Name _____

Date _____

INTRODUCTION: Read this article. Using your own words, answer the questions at the end of the article.

Nature's Harmony

In *The Wizard of Oz*, Dorothy and her friends, as they entered the forest, were afraid of meeting lions and tigers and bears. In nature one would never find these three animals living in the same place. In many ways they are too much alike and their needs are too similar to share the same habitat. A habitat is the place where a plant or animal lives. In every habitat there are particular jobs that an organism must perform. Different plants and animals perform the same function in different habitats. A lion, a tiger, a shark, and a polar bear perform the same kind of job in different places. Each of them is a large predator that eats other animals in its habitat.

We often think of predators as cruel, frightening animals that eat cute little animals or even people. When we hear the story of the three little pigs we think of the "big bad wolf" as a villain for wanting to do his job, eat pigs. However, predators are important to their habitats, because they keep the prey populations that they eat from growing too large. They kill the weakest animals in the prey population, often the ill or the old or the infirm. If the predatory population is reduced unnaturally, such as when humans hunt them, the size of the prey population grows too big. When this happens, there is not enough food or nesting sites to support the large prey population. As a result, the prey die in a crueler manner than if they had been killed and eaten by a predator. In a habitat an important balance is maintained by the interactions between different populations. The predator-prey relationship is one such interaction. Most organisms have natural enemies that keep their populations from growing too large.

When we bring an organism from one habitat to another, we often disrupt this balance. If the natural checks on a population are not present, the population grows too big. Many times in the past, humans have brought plants or animals from one habitat to another, either accidentally or on purpose, with disastrous results. Rabbits were introduced to Australia, where they had no natural enemies. These "cute" animals became an uncontrolled population — a major pest that ravaged much of the farmers' grazing land. Other such examples include the introduction of the Japanese beetle to the United States and African bees to South America.

Why don't lions, tigers, and bears live in the same habitat? If we look at the lion, tiger, shark ,or polar bear, we could find some important similarities between them such, as the shape and size of their teeth. An animal must have the equipment to do its particular job. The lion, the tiger, and the polar bear must each have sharp, pointed teeth to tear meat from its prey and sharp claws to tear open and hold down its prey. Certain structural forms are necessary for the particular functions that the organism must perform. We say that form follows function. By this we mean that the form an animal takes must meet the needs of the functions it performs. We expect animals that do similar jobs to have basic similarities. Because these animal perform their jobs in different places they must also be different. The lion is tan like the grass on the African plains where it lives. The tiger is striped like the forest of India. The polar bear is white like the snow on which it hunts. The animal must be built specifically for its particular habitat. The polar bear, the tiger, and the lion must each be able to blend with its environment, so that it can sneak up on its prey without being seen. Because they live in different habitats, they look different; each is able to blend with its particular habitat. The polar bear would be visible if it were hunting on a grassland. It would also be too warm. Similarly, a lion or tiger would stand out on an ice field and would probably freeze.

When two similar animals occupy the same habitat, they compete with each other until only one of them remains. One of the animals may change to perform a somewhat different job, perhaps eat different animals or breed at a different time of the year, but two animals that perform the same job cannot survive in the same habitat. The animal that is best suited to the particular habitat will survive, while the other will die.

The natural balance that exists in any habitat is a very delicate one. Often when we humans interfere, we disrupt this harmony. During our history we have done many things to destroy the delicate balance in nature. We have hunted some species to extinction. We have introduced species to foreign habitats, thus unbalancing them. We have destroyed habitats by replacing them with civilization. Expecting to find lions, tigers, and bears in the same place is symbolic of our lack of understanding of nature. We must learn to understand the consequences of our actions before we disrupt nature. Scientists say that there are millions of species of organisms in the world that have not been discovered yet. If we continue to destroy habitats, we may never discover them, for they will have become extinct.

QUESTIONS

1. What is a habitat?

    _____

    _____

2. How is a polar bear adapted to its environment?

    _____

    _____

3. In what ways are lions and tigers similar to polar bears? Why?

    _____

    _____

4. In what ways are lions and tigers different? Why do you think this is so?

    _____

    _____

5. What would happen to an animal population if its natural enemies were killed?

    _____

    _____

6. How has man disrupted the balance of nature?

    _____

    _____

7. What is meant by "Form follows function"?

    _____

    _____

8. What are some natural enemies of harmful insects?

    _____

    _____

9. Why are there laws regulating the importation of foreign species?

    _____

    _____

Student Page –
Testing the pH of Water

Name _____

Date _____

DESCRIPTION:

1. Describe how you tested the water samples for pH.

     _____

     _____

2. Describe the results of the test.

     _____

     _____

     _____

QUESTIONS:

1. What does pH indicate?

     _____

     _____

2. Why is it important to know the pH of water?

     _____

     _____

3. What causes the pH of rainwater to drop?

     _____

     _____

4. What is acid rain?

     _____

     _____

5. What causes acid rain?

     _____

     _____

Student Page –
Acid–Base Indicators

Name _____

Date _____

DESCRIPTION: List each of the indicators you observed and their color in an acid and in a base.

_____

_____

_____

_____

_____

_____

_____

QUESTIONS:

1. Which indicator would be best to test pH?

_____

_____

2. What does pH measure?

_____

3. When have you come across the term *pH*?

_____

_____

4. List some common acids.

_____

_____

5. List some common bases.

_____

_____

_____

Student Page –
Cabbage Juice Indicator

Name _____

Date _____

DESCRIPTION: Describe the color of the cabbage juice at each pH.

_____

_____

_____

_____

_____

_____

_____

_____

QUESTIONS:

1. Why does cabbage juice change color?

_____

_____

2. Certain plants will produce either pink or blue flowers depending on
   the pH of the soil. How can you account for this?

_____

_____

3. How can you test the pH of the soil?

_____

_____

4. Would you consider the pH of the soil part of the physical environment of a plant? Explain your answer.

_____

_____

Student Page –   Name _____
Acid Rain   Date _____

DESCRIPTION:

1. Describe the color in each of the three flasks.

    _____

    _____

2. After burning sulfur in the test flask which standard was its color
    like? What does this tell you about the effect of burning sulfur on
    water?

    _____

    _____

QUESTIONS:

1. What is acid rain?

    _____

    _____

2. How does the burning of high–sulfur coal cause acid rain?

    _____

    _____

3. Where does the sulfur dioxide combine with water to produce acid
    rain?

    _____

    _____

4. Why is acid rain considered harmful to the environment?

    _____

    _____

5. How can we prevent the formation of acid rain?

    _____

    _____

    _____

Student Page –
Erosion of Soil

Name _____

Date _____

DESCRIPTION: Describe this demonstration of erosion.

_____

_____

_____

_____

_____

_____

QUESTIONS:

1. What causes the erosion of soil?

_____

_____

2. What can be done to stop erosion from occurring?

_____

_____

3. When large tracts of trees are cut down what happens to the soil?

_____

_____

4. What can be done to prevent soil erosion after trees are cut down?

_____

_____

**Student Page –
Soil Cover**

Name _____

Date _____

DESCRIPTION: Describe this demonstration.

_____

_____

_____

_____

_____

_____

_____

_____

QUESTIONS:

1. Why is soil cover important?

_____

_____

2. What kinds of plants are used as soil cover?

_____

_____

3. What happens if soil cover is not used?

_____

_____

Acid Rain

Name _____

Date _____

INTRODUCTION: Acid rain is the name we give, not just rain, but to any precipitation that is more acidic than normal. We measure the acidity of rainwater or of any solution on a scale called *pH* a term you may have come across before. The term *pH* means "hydrogen power," because all acids contain the hydrogen ion. The pH scale goes from 0 to 14; the lower the pH value on the scale, the more acidic is the solution. A pH of 0 is very acidic, a pH of 14 is very basic, and a pH of 7 is neutral.

The pH of rainwater is normally between 5 and 7. Acid rain can be defined as any precipitation with a pH below 5. Rain becomes acid rain when it absorbs acids of nitrogen and sulfur from the atmosphere. When we burn fuels that contain sulfur or nitrogen, we add oxides of these elements to the atmosphere. These oxides combine with water in the atmosphere to produce acid rain.

The effects of acid rain are felt in lakes and forests, where animals and plants are harmed by the acid. Many organisms have a low tolerance for acids and are killed by the change in pH. Acid rain falling on a lake in the eastern United States changes the lake by making it more and more acidic. In this activity you are going to measure the pH of lake water taken from different lakes, as well as rainwater and tap water.

EQUIPMENT AND MATERIALS:

6 water samples
6 stirring rods

Glass plate
Hydrion paper with color
   chart

PROCEDURE:

1.   Place a strip of Hydrion paper on the glass plate. Dip a clean stirring rod into the first sample and touch it to the Hydrion paper. Compare the color of the paper with the color chart to determine the pH of the sample. Record the name of the sample and its pH in the data table.

2.   For each water sample, repeat the procedure described in step 1.

DATA TABLE

Sample	Name	pH
1		
2		
3		
4		
5		
6		

CONCLUSIONS:

1.   Which sample was the most acidic?

     _____

2.   Which sample was the least acidic?

     _____

QUESTIONS:

1.   How does a lake become acidified?

     _____

     _____

2.   If a solution has a pH of 3 and another has a pH of 5, which is the
     more acidic? Explain your answer.

     _____

     _____

3.   What are the main sources of acid rain?

     _____

     _____

4.   Why might acid precipitation be a better name than acid rain?

     _____

     _____

5. How is a lake affected by acid rain?

_____

_____

SUGGESTIONS FOR FURTHER STUDY:

- Try adding sodium bicarbonate to the acidified water to see how it affects the pH of the water.